FACING CANCER
WITHOUT
GOD

MATT L. MILLER

JULY 10, 1963 – JANUARY 25, 2010

EDITED BY

KERMIT MOYER
NATALIE ROSS MILLER

FORWARD PRESS
LOS ANGELES

ALSO BY MATT MILLER

Digital Watermarking

Cox, Miller, and Bloom. 2002.
Morgan Kaufmann Publ., Academic Press,
a Harcourt Science and Technology Company

COPYEDITING:
Kate Zentall, Los Angeles CA

DESIGN AND COVER ART:
Glenn Wong, GW Graphic Works, Los Angeles CA

ISBN 978-0-9668573-1-3 (Printed Version)
ISBN 978-0-9668573-2-0 (E-Book Version)

FORWARD PRESS
3594 Ocean View Avenue
Los Angeles, CA 90066

CONTENTS

A WORD ABOUT MATT

Matt always wanted to be a hero. As the family story goes, one day when he was a teenager he answered the front door to a pair of Jehovah's Witnesses. "Good morning," one of the ladies said, launching into their prepared message, "do you believe that one man can change the world?" Matt, genially and without hesitation, replied, "I'm sure as hell gonna try!"

He grew to be a respected and passionate computer programmer who hoped to do things that mattered. Unfortunately, lung cancer cut him off much too early. In the two-plus years between his diagnosis and his death in 2010, he spent time putting his thoughts down on paper, principally to leave a firsthand record for his wife and daughters. Friends who read early drafts convinced him that his slightly off-kilter take on the mysteries of existence and the sources of solace for an atheist deserved a wider audience. It has taken the family time to heal before we could gather up his notes and put them together in readable form.

The result is the book you hold here.

NRM
Cape Cod

ACKNOWLEDGMENTS

There is a substantial gulf between believing that Matt's writings deserved a wider readership than the immediate family and actually getting them pulled together and edited. The encouragement, early on, of Matt's friends Peter Brown and Christian Wildberg fired up Matt to keep writing as his death approached. The unfinished manuscript was shown to Daniel Mendelsohn, whose extraordinarily positive response strengthened our resolve but whose detailed suggestions for revisions proved daunting. In the emotional wake of Matt's death the task seemed insurmountable, and the project languished.

Eventually it was borne in on me, Matt's mother, that I was the logical person to take on the task. I had the time, and I must thank Richard Whalen for convincing me that I had the ability. I took the manuscript as far as I could and then stalled. Enter Kermit Moyer, writer and teacher, who fell in love with the project and did the heavy lifting of re-arranging the notes into a whole. Through the good offices of Barbara Ravage—always prodding me to keep at it—I met Kate Zentall, whose injection of energy, passion, and expertise brought us to the finish line. And thanks to

Glenn Wong for his thoughtful and caring design.

Thank you all.

I am eternally grateful to Giedre, Matt's wife, for her emotional support and for clarifying some history, as well as to Matt's brother and sister, whose love and encouragement have meant so much.

Most of all I thank my husband, Lorimer, who read every single permutation of this testament and kept me from meddling too much with Matt's unique voice.

SCIENCE

When Adam bit the apple
God took away the tree.
But Adam didn't wallow
In hopeless misery.
He finished up the apple
And planted all the seeds.
Now Adam has an orchard
Where God had had a tree.

MLM
1979

THE BIG CHANGE

LIKE MOST PEOPLE, I'VE LIVED most of my life in the shallow end of the pool. I've splashed around, doing things that seemed serious—meeting deadlines at work, traveling to distant places, making financial decisions, falling in and out of love. I've amused myself with what seemed to be the grand topics of history, philosophy, science, and religion. I've thought what I thought were deep thoughts. But all the while I had my feet safely planted on the bottom and my head well above the waterline. Then one day a brief conversation with a doctor dragged me into the deep end, and suddenly I had to find out whether I knew how to swim.

From that day to this, my decisions have not merely seemed serious, they've been literally matters of life and death. Those supposedly deep thoughts are no longer academic amusements; they've had to keep me afloat through truly terrifying times. They've had to help me keep my nerve as I underwent dangerous medical procedures. They've had to keep me sane through long, sleepless, cavernous nights. And hardest of all, they've had to keep me getting up every morning, brushing my teeth, getting dressed, eating, taking

1

my pills, and attending to such minutia while all the time faced with the threat that I may very soon leave my two daughters fatherless and my wife a widow.

On the day of my diagnosis, I became much more particular about what to spend my time on—what conversations to have, what movies and TV to watch, what books to read, and so on. When you're in water over your head, anything that doesn't look like a life preserver becomes singularly uninteresting. What I was after fell into three basic categories: I wanted information, but only in forms I could use, from sources I trusted, and in amounts that wouldn't terrify me. I wanted escape, but it had to be flavored to my taste, capable of taking my mind off the situation for a couple of hours and giving it a rest. And I wanted encouragement, but it had to be the right type of encouragement. Few things are more discouraging than encouragement that doesn't encourage.

As I write this, I am imagining a very specific reader: an atheist with cancer. This means I assume that, like me, you believe that God, Allah, Yahweh, Vishnu, Zeus, Baal, the Man in the Moon, and Mickey Mouse are all equally fictitious. I assume also that, like me, you have been diagnosed with this wretched and scary disease. If you're an atheist with some wretched and scary disease other than cancer, or an atheist facing some wretched and scary crisis other than a disease, I hope you'll be able to relate to the thoughts I'm writing here. Perhaps you fall into a group for whom the physical crisis being faced has precipitated a crisis of faith—those who always thought themselves believers but when told the bad news from the doctor suddenly began to question God's love. I hope people in this fix might pick up a book that features "without God" in the title to take a peek at how things would look if they just gave up on faith entirely. On a wider scale, I imagine (*fantasize* might be a more appropriate word) that there could be some interest in this book among people who are not in crisis—atheists who want to look at ways of facing crisis in a godless universe, or theists who are wise enough to know there *are* such things as atheists in foxholes and who want to learn about how we cope.

In the first decade of the 21st century, a number of books on atheism suddenly appeared on bestseller lists, most notably Sam Harris's *The End of Faith*, Richard Dawkins's *The God Delusion*, and Christopher Hitchens's *God Is Not Great*. These books, by and large, try to convince readers that faith in God is a bad idea. I call them God-bashing books. It's true that I'm already part of the choir they preach to, but I've enjoyed them all greatly because they gave me a sense of camaraderie while I was going through chemotherapy.

But what I'm writing here is not a God-bashing book, and it's a good thing too, because I'm not the least bit qualified to write one. To write a decent God-basher, I'd have to plow through the whole damned Bible, the Koran, probably the Bhagavad Gita, the Book of Mormon, and maybe even Dianetics for good measure. You can't formulate a sound argument against something unless you've studied it thoroughly, and I'm not about to waste the time

I have left on such a project. Now, I can hear believers saying, "Ah, if he'd only read [fill in the blank], he'd see the light and realize the Truth." But believers tend to dismiss all the books *except their own*. How many Christians dismiss the Bhagavad Gita or Dianetics without reading them through? That's the same thing I'm doing, except I'm dismissing *all* these books without reading them through. I've read and heard enough to know that none of them seems at all realistic.

Over the centuries a body of Western philosophy and science has grown up around atheism, skepticism, and existentialism. Unlike most Americans, I was raised from childhood to believe this philosophy—or rather, to believe in the process by which it was conceived, the process of evidentiary reasoning. It's a process that differs from the religious practice of faith in that it is exclusively focused on narrowing one's beliefs down to demonstrable truths. The question I face, in facing cancer, is whether a universe composed only of these demonstrable truths, and only ever believed on condition of continued demonstration, can offer me the emotional support I need to carry on. So far the answer has been yes. I don't think I've had more trouble than some of the believers I've seen around me. And I've never had to wonder why a God who loved me could do such a cruel thing as give me this disease.

I may lack a deep knowledge of theological arcana, but it's impossible for any American these days to avoid seeing what religion means to people. Shelves in bookstores are filled with religious guidance for those up against all sorts of hardships. Countless TV shows and movies tell stories of people receiving affirmations of their faith. It sometimes seems as if every athlete, every politician, every average Joe who suffers hard times and ends up on the news—basically everyone in America who finds a soapbox and an audience—does not hesitate to go on at length about the importance of their faith in God. Well, this book is my soapbox. I've been dealing with some pretty hard times of my own, and I want to talk about the importance of my disbelief in God. Or rather, I want to talk about the things I do believe in: my own will to carry on, love of my wife and daughters, love of art, science, and humor, to name a few. In these incontrovertible aspects of human experience I find everything I've heard believers claim they get from religion: courage, love, solace, hope, purpose.

□   □   □

AN UGLY CT SCAN

On April 2, 2007, I was living in suburban New Jersey, with a nice little house, a promising career, a lovely wife who was just embarking on her own promising career, and two ridiculously beautiful daughters. It was a Monday, my wife, Giedre's, birthday, and spring was in the air. Plus, it was the first day of a school break for Fia and Ada, and we'd enrolled them in a day camp at the local Y. That morning I got them ready, piled them into the car, and drove them to the Y, only to discover I was supposed to pack lunches for them. So I left the kids there, drove home again, made some lunches, drove to the Y a second time, and found Ada at the reception desk trying to help the counselors find my cell phone number. I'd hardly had time to realize that something was wrong before several counselors dragged me into the front office. There was Fia, covered in tears and blood. In the short time that it had taken me to pack the lunches, she'd managed to smash her two front teeth. I tried to reassure her by telling her that this was actually something of a tradition in my family, both my siblings having smashed their teeth when they were kids. My sister ran into a wall, and my brother broke a tooth in choir practice (yes, he was an atheist in a church choir—I always tell people he fell flat on a sharp note). Fia managed a wan smile at this, but I think the busted teeth and fat lip really had her preoccupied.

There ensued one of those days of complex parental logistics, driving from town to town, calling doctors and insurance companies, and trying to coordinate with Giedre so that she could take over and I could finally get to work. At last I got to the office, many hours later than intended.

I had one other chore to attend to. I'd had a nagging cough for several months, and after a few rounds of antibiotics had failed to rid me of it I'd seen a pulmonologist, who'd sent me for a CT scan the preceding Friday. When I got the scan, the technicians told me that if they found anything bad they'd get in touch with me right away. I hadn't heard anything all weekend, so I figured everything was OK. But just for the sake of completeness, I had to call and get the results.

In addition to the cough, I'd been having a couple of

other problems, which had received separate diagnoses. There were bouts of intense back pain, but hey, what 40-something guy doesn't have occasional bouts of back pain? I also had a blind spot in my left eye, which was freaky, but this had been diagnosed as something called a central serous retinopathy (CSR), which isn't serious and usually goes away by itself.

I called the pulmonologist's office and left a message. They called back and said the doctor liked to give results in person, so we made an appointment for late that afternoon. I managed to get in a few hours of work before I took off to meet him. I chatted with the receptionist and the nurse and settled in to the examination room to await the doctor. It was annoying to have to spend so much time hanging around doctors' offices.

When the doctor came in, he looked pretty down. The way I remember it, he didn't look me in the eye. He sat down and began listing the problems in my scan: There was a mass in the lung, swollen lymph nodes everywhere, and several "worrisome" growths on my spine and ribs and sternum. The center lobe in my lung was completely collapsed, and the mass was butted up against it, making it impossible to tell how large the mass was. But they could tell it was big. "This was," said the doc, staring gravely into his notes, "an ugly CT scan."

There's a scene in the Steve Martin movie *The Lonely Guy* in which Martin's character comes home to find his girlfriend in bed with another guy. Instead of screaming at them or throwing them out or anything of that nature, he just goes about his normal routine. Checking his mail. Asking his girlfriend how her day was. Finally, the girlfriend cries out in frustration, "I don't believe you—you come home, you find me in bed with another man, and you act as if nothing's going on!" Martin replies, "I've never been in a situation like this before. I don't know how to handle it."

Well, I'd never been in a situation like this before either, and I didn't know how to handle it.

When the doctor told me it was an ugly CT, I honestly didn't know what to think. So if, during the following few moments, I seemed overly cool, it was not due to any kind of heroism. It was just that I'd drawn a complete emotional blank.

I said, "Well, that sucks."

"Yes," replied my pulmonologist, hardly daring to look up from his notes. "It sucks."

He halfheartedly poked a couple of spots on my rib cage, asking whether it hurt. It didn't. He told me there was a long list of possible diagnoses. It might be lung cancer. It might be lymphoma. And it might be any number of other things, many of them minor. But clearly he was padding the list. This was almost certainly something extremely bad. The minor explanations were long shots at best. What wasn't clear was whether he was padding the list for my sake or for his.

At some point, maybe in response to a question on my part, he told me that some types of lymphoma were curable.

Wait ... what? Some types of lymphoma were curable?

So lung cancer and other types of lymphoma were ... uh ... not?

That was the point at which it began to sink in just what serious trouble I was in.

I made an appointment for a bronchoscopy in a couple of days. The results would be back from the lab in about a week, and that would nail down the diagnosis. In the meantime, I'd have to wait. Just before I left, I asked the doctor whether the problem in my eye might have anything to do with the stuff in the CT scan. He said no, without hesitation.

The exact order of events for the rest of that day isn't clear in my memory. I know I managed to call Giedre before I got home. I know I bought flowers for her birthday, and when I gave them to her it seemed almost cruel—making any reference at all to the idea that this was supposed to be a happy day just seemed to make things worse. I called my parents and my brother and sister, and within a few days' time they all traveled to be with me in Princeton. I also called my ophthalmologist, Dr. Amy Kotecha, to ask the same question that the pulmonologist had answered so confidently in the negative. She contradicted him, saying it was certainly possible that the thing in my eye was a tumor, and she'd like to take another look at it.

My oldest daughter, Fia, is twelve as I write this. She is learning to play the guitar. She whipped through the Harry Potter books and likes to read about Greek mythology. Ada is nine. Like her physicist grandfather (my father), she loves science and helps her big sister with her math homework. They're both bright and strong-minded, like their mother. Giedre and I have always included them in our ups and downs. Giedre in particular feels deeply committed to being completely open with them about my illness. In her own case, when she was in her early teens and her mother contracted cancer and subsequently died of it, Giedre and her siblings were left in the dark about why their mother would disappear from time to time (for hospital stays) or why she was so tired. They found out she was seriously ill only when she died. So it was imperative to us that Fia and Ada know from the start what was going on. They knew, of course, that I was seeing a doctor about my cough, and they were in the room when I had to tell Giedre the bad news. We have not spared them any details. It's impressive how they have taken it in stride, assuming—as children will—that I will be cured.

For a few days, my family and I tried to convince ourselves it was lymphoma, which at least was curable. Even if it wasn't, by this point I'd learned that the incurable lymphomas were usually more controllable than late-stage lung cancer (i.e. lung cancer that had spread to the bones and eyes). It wasn't that unusual for incurable lymphoma patients to live for decades with frequent therapies. Lung cancer, on the other hand … Well, I didn't want to think about that, but I was struck by what it said about my condition that while most people would be horrified to learn they had lymphoma, that was exactly the news I was longing to hear.

Then I went to see Dr. Kotecha, and she was the first

to peg the diagnosis. She'd mostly seen pictures of these things in books; only once, briefly, as a student, had she seen one in real life. But she was fairly certain now that what she saw in my eye was a metastasis from a solid-tumor carcinoma. Given everything else we knew, that meant just one thing: lung cancer.

It was Easter weekend when the results from the biopsy confirmed Dr. Kotecha's diagnosis. The girls mostly stayed in their room. My sister, Kate, was distraught. Giedre was frantic but went into action, calling a Lithuanian relative who worked at Sloan-Kettering and getting names and entrées to the right doctors. My parents and brother held it together, helping by taking calls and making notes of names and phone numbers. At Sloan-Kettering we made contact with Dr. Vincent Miller, an expert on lung cancer in people who've never smoked, and through him we got onto a local oncologist, Dr. John Sierocki. I also contacted an ophthalmic oncologist at Sloan-Kettering, Dr. David Abramson. It was an emotional and tumultuous few days, and then my new life began.

I was scanned up one side and down the other. I found out that my back pain was the result of a three-inch tumor in the middle of my spine, and various pains I'd felt in my ribs were the result of tumors in those bones. I had a small, suspicious lesion in my brain, but it wasn't clear whether that was a tumor or something that had always been there. Other than that, the rest of my body was still clean. My liver, kidneys, heart, digestive system, neck, and all the bones outside my torso were still OK.

During the weeks it took to prepare for my treatment, my symptoms progressed rapidly. I lost almost all sight in my left eye; only a sliver of peripheral vision remained. The back pain became almost crippling; I was still able to walk, but only very slowly, and it hurt like hell. And the cough got to the point where I couldn't really carry on a conversation or sleep through the night. Of course, sleeping through the night wasn't much of an option anyway. If you've been through this, you probably know what I'm talking about. The days are almost bearable—people are awake, there's daylight outside, things to be done, doctors to be seen, scans to be taken, plans to be made. At night, there's … nothing. Nothing but that one thing on your mind.

I don't care what religion you follow or what philosophical world-view you take, I cannot believe there is any solace to be had in those first few nights. Distraction is the best you can hope for. Philosophical or religious solace can only come later, after the news has sunk in, after the fact of having cancer has become an integral part of your inner life. I'm deeply suspicious of anyone who has received a diagnosis like mine and who claims not to have felt utterly bereft.

As for me, I took to spending the nights on the couch in the living room with the TV on. We put a mattress on the floor, and each night either my brother or Giedre, whoever was feeling up to it, kept me company. We'd chat until whoever was with me fell asleep, and then I'd spend several hours flipping channels. Strangely, I found I favored watching horror movies, maybe because they're fake; the people in them are actors, the dangers just special effects. I think I also had some newfound fascination with the forms of human fear—fear of death, of course, but also fear of becoming evil, or fear of knowing too much about the future. Eventually I'd doze off a little, interrupted periodically by coughing. The sounds of voices on the TV and of breathing beside me reassured me that life would go on. Daybreak once again brought light and an awakening family and a schedule of events and possibilities.

The first doctors who had delivered the news—my GP, my pulmonologist, and Dr. Kotecha—couldn't hide their discouragement at what they had to say. Things were different when I started dealing with the experts in lung cancer, Doctors Sierocki, Miller, and Abramson. My diagnosis had come at a moment of great excitement in the field. New drugs and treatments were finally beginning to break through an initial barrier that these guys had been banging their heads against for decades. The change hadn't shown up in the statistics yet; the drugs were too new and they worked on too few patients, but more and more people who in the past could not have been expected to live more than a few months were now making it through a year or two. In particular, Dr. Miller, along with some other researchers, had recently found that a particular drug, Tarceva, had a good chance of working on people who had never smoked. When it worked, it usually lasted a couple of years before the cancer evolved a resistance to it, so he said to me, "This should keep you alive for two or three years, and by then we'll know what to do next."

He was definitely right about the first part. But he was wrong about how long it would take for him and other researchers to figure out what to do next. In my case, they still don't quite know what they're doing.

I was started on a combination of old-fashioned, make-your-hair-fall-out cytotoxic chemo and Tarceva. For various reasons I had to start the cytotoxic chemo first. But when I began taking Tarceva, a single daily pill, the results were spectacular. Within days, literally, I began to regain some vision in my left eye. The first thing I was able to read with it—and I'm not making this up—was a street sign down the block from my house: "Clearview Avenue." Within a month or so, my vision in that eye was almost normal. Sometimes now I close the other eye while I'm reading or writing, just to gloat. Or while I'm taking a walk on a sunny day, I'll shut my good eye to see the world anew through the other. I can tell you there is absolutely nothing as beautiful as sunlight seen glinting off tree leaves through a once-blind eye.

A week or two into the combined treatment, Dr. Sierocki suggested I try going off the painkillers I was taking for my back. The back pain was completely gone. The cough disappeared gradually.

Scans and measurements backed up these results. The tumor in my eye was gone, the only distortions in my vision coming from scarring it left behind. The tumor in my lung was undetectable. The tumors in my bones had shrunk to the point where they'd bother me only a little in bad weather, though the bigger ones were still alive. And I didn't have too hard a time with the cytotoxic chemo. Don't get me wrong; it wasn't fun. I felt pretty sick almost all the time and often spent whole days in bed. I lost my hair and sense of taste. The worst was that I had five epileptic seizures during the course of the treatment. But many patients have it far worse than I did. I never threw up. And after the treatment was over, I recovered pretty quickly. The only lasting side effects have been a little loss of feeling in a couple of toes and a reduced interest in sweets.

For most of 2007 and 2008, I was essentially healthy. I was able to travel—for work to Japan and for pleasure to Lithuania and Denmark. I was able to drive as of a year from the most recent seizure. I wasn't in any pain. The only concrete effects the disease had on my life were mountains of daily pills, frequent doctor visits, and bouts of scanning every several months, each of which brought a short period of uncertainty and fear until we got the results.

Finally, however, the fears began to be realized. First, the disease spread into my pelvis. I could feel it there: pains in my keester when I sat too long, a sensation my brother called "tired butt syndrome." Later, small tumors began cropping up in my brain like popcorn. These were asymptomatic, but all my doctors were concerned about them. By the time there were more than eight, Dr. Sierocki insisted that I had to have whole-brain radiation, and I could tell he didn't think my prognosis was very good. After the radiation was over, I was elated that I could still think clearly, but the pain in my pelvis really took off. No painkiller could control it, and for a couple of weeks I was once again bedridden. It was time for some new chemo.

At the moment I'm writing this paragraph I'm in the middle of that new round of chemo. This time the drugs I'm on are far milder, and the only significant side effect is weakness. I'm no longer bedridden, I go to work every day, all the pain is gone (except for occasional leg cramps that are probably just due to weakness), and best of all, the last MRI of my brain showed no tumors.

The disappearance of my brain tumors, coming so soon after my radiation therapy, was a great surprise to all my doctors. These were the tumors that had them most worried, and they really weren't expected to go away so quickly, if at all. What's going to happen next is anybody's guess. Sometimes, when tumors disappear quickly, they stay away for a long time; sometimes they come roaring back a short time later, harder to eradicate than ever. There's no statistical precedent on which to base a prediction. So now I'm just living day to day.

□   □   □

THE 800-POUND GORILLA

From the moment the doctors first gave me the news of my diagnosis, it has been virtually impossible to get the topic completely out of my head. Whatever the time of day, wherever I am, whatever I'm doing, there's always that proverbial 800-pound gorilla in the room, pestering me with one constant message: *You might die soon.*

In the first several days, it often reached the point of absurdity. Attempts by my friends and family to distract me with lighter topics was like the buzzing of faraway bees. I grew so exhausted trying to form coherent thoughts about the disease that at times I found myself mindlessly reciting *cancer, cancer, cancer* in my head ad nauseam.

As I prepared for treatment and had more practical tasks available to dive into and get done, these thoughts became easier to deal with. The gorilla backed off a bit, but my cancer is not curable, so I've never gone all the way back to the shallow end of the pool. Thanks to a spectacular response to Tarceva, my life has been near-normal lately, although there are always those alarms, some true, some false, to remind me of where I am. In this treading-water state, I have found it possible to write for long stretches, especially after I've had some crisis or other and things appear to be going well again.

When a doctor grabs you by the face and forces you to look at your mortality, you're flooded with a wave of questions that most of us spend our time trying to ignore, questions that seem to be answered for most people by religion. But given my background, the kinds of answers I tend toward have nothing to do with anything supernatural. I'm not sure dwelling on these questions now really helps me, but I am sure it's unavoidable, so I have no choice but to go ahead and discuss them one by one.

□ □ □

ALL IN THE FAMILY

IF I PERSISTED IN THINKING that my cancer was not necessarily a death sentence, it was due in large part to the fact that many years earlier both my parents had survived cancer: Mom had survived ovarian cancer, and Dad had survived first bladder cancer and then prostate cancer. Also rooted firmly in family history was my atheism, a tradition of secularism that went back several generations.

I come from what strikes me as extremely colorful lineage, and although I know far too little about many of my ancestors to do them justice, especially in a book where the focus is on other things, I'd nevertheless like to try to give some sense of where I come from and how I got to be the way I am.

My dad, Gabriel Lorimer Miller, was born on January 18, 1928, when my English grandparents, both actors at the time, were in New York City. This meant that though the family returned to London a few years later, he had dual U.S./British citizenship.

Dad continued in the intellectual tradition of the family but eschewed theater and literature. Instead, he became an experimental nuclear physicist. In fact, for most of my life it was well nigh impossible to drag him to a play or a movie. My mom, Natalie Stanton Coffin—stage name Natalie Ross—was the actress in my family, and how my parents met is something of a story. She grew up in Pasadena, California, dreaming of becoming a star. At first, like any California kid, she dreamed of movies, but as she became more serious she turned her attention to the stage. After majoring in drama at the University of Washington, she got a Fulbright scholarship to continue her studies at the Royal Academy of Dramatic Art (RADA) in London. My mom's favorite teacher at RADA was none other than the man who would become my grandfather, Hugh Miller. Hugh occasionally had some of his students come to his flat for tea, and Mom's turn duly came. She met Hugh's wife, Olga, and his daughter, Sonya, and learned that he had two sons: Jonathan, off at Oxford, and Lorimer, getting his PhD in physics at the University of London, and who, be it noted, might well have been in the flat at the time but stayed resolutely in his room studying. I guess he figured if the guests were lightweight enough to be students of acting, he wasn't interested. It wasn't until some six years later, when both sons were working in New York, that the two finally met. As luck would have it, Hugh and Olga came over for a visit and Jonathan took them to see a friend in a showcase of *The Way of the World*, in which Mom was playing the lead. There was a happy reunion of teacher and student, but there was no chemistry between Mom and Jonathan, and older brother Lorimer, then working at Brookhaven National Labs on Long Island, once again passed on the theater. Nonetheless, before Jonathan left to go back to London, he enthusiastically recommended to Lorimer that he look up Natalie Ross.

Mom was quite a catch at the time—young, blond, and gorgeous, playing the lead role of Connie in Neil Simon's first Broadway hit, *Come Blow Your Horn*. And I don't know what happened to that shy guy who wouldn't come out of his room when my grandfather held an open house for his students, but by the time he met my mom, he had … presence. When he walked into a room, everybody knew it. He would come in with a bad joke and an infectious laugh and the whole atmosphere would change. When he and Mom were courting, he would sometimes pick her up backstage after the show. Outside the stage door would be a bunch of fans seeking autographs. Mom still complains that many people would ask Dad for his autograph, thinking a guy that electrifying must be some sort of star, and she complains even more about how many autographs he would actually go ahead and sign. He addressed everything with the same sort of joie de vivre, including religious matters. Guests in our house had to have thick skins where religion was concerned, because the idea of politely avoiding the subject never occurred to Dad. As far as he was concerned, every belief was to be challenged. It was grand sport. He could quote chapter and verse of the Bible with the best of them, and he'd read virtually every other major book of scripture.

But it was my great-grandfather, Isaac Johan Katzin, my father's mother's father, who started it all. His daughter,

Olga, dominated my father's family, and my dad and uncle grew up ardent unbelievers. My information about my great-grandfather Johan Katzin is both partial and unreliable, but I know that he was from either Plunge or Palanga, Lithuania, and that his family was murdered by the Nazis, but he himself had left well before World War I, when he was just a teenager, and had gone to Holland to seek his fortune. In Amsterdam he got into the diamond trade and did rather well, until (so I've heard) he had his fortune tied up in a small but highly valuable shipment of diamonds that he somehow lost on the streets of Amsterdam. Figuring the diamond trade was not for him, he then headed for South Africa and started a business in Cape Town doing the laundry of ships sailing round the tip of Africa. This being the days before the Suez Canal, the business proved very profitable, and he ended up with a much bigger and safer fortune than he would ever have gained in diamonds. Somewhere along the way he married one Mathilda Litoun, the daughter of a London innkeeper. I know virtually nothing about Mathilda except that she was also Jewish, and her family was originally from Prague. The marriage, and the fact that South Africa was a British colony, meant that the family always had one foot in Africa and the other in England.

I've been told that Isaac Johan Katzin was very superstitious, a believer in the fortune-telling power of dreams and premonitions. He was in a shipwreck and lost a leg at some point, which apparently left him very attentive to signs and auguries for the rest of his life. Nevertheless, he

is the one who abandoned religion. The story has it that
he came to the decision fairly late in his life, when he was
older than I am now. He simply announced one day that
this was the end of religion for the Katzins, then took all
the paraphernalia—yarmulkas, shawls, Bibles—and pitched
them out the window. If this is true, it must have been a
spectacular scene, but I'm sorry to say I don't have any idea
what lay behind it. All I know is, with a few notable ex-
ceptions, his descendants have become increasingly irreli-
gious over the generations.

Johan and Mathilda had seven children—three sons
and four daughters—all of whom seem to have led remark-
able lives. Alfred, for example, was a colonel during
World War II and later became an undersecretary to Dag
Hammarskjöld at the United Nations. Winifred married
the president of the Red Cross, spent the whole of World
War II as his secretary in Switzerland, and after his death
used her multilingual skills in becoming a successful
translator of European plays into English.

And then there's my grandmother, Olga. The adjective
that seems to have come first to the mind of anyone who
knew her at all well is *fearsome*. She struck terror into her
two daughters-in-law. And on the web I found that "fearsome woman" were the words used to describe her by an
actor who had met her in New York in the '20s.

It wasn't just her character that made her fearsome, it
was her intellect. She started her career in the theater,
writing and acting. This was where she got together with
my grandfather, Hugh Miller, an English actor from the

Scottish border who had a healthy career in movies, theater, and teaching at RADA. I've found some old reviews of their early performances together when Olga was still acting, and a few of his performances are preserved on film, mostly corny old black-and-white flicks like *Bulldog Drummond at Bay*. He also had cameos in two major movies, *Lawrence of Arabia* and *Dr. Zhivago*, where his main role was behind the camera as acting coach. The reviews of his performances were always good; hers, less so. Hugh once confided to my mother that to be an actor one shouldn't be overly intellectual, which Olga apparently was. As a writer, however, she was a force, and though she started out writing plays, it was as a satirical poet that she came into her own. Throughout World War II, she wrote political satire for *The New Statesman* and *Nation* under the pen name Sagittarius and also published several bound volumes of poetry. My father tells of a day near the end of the war when the family was gathered round the breakfast table reading the London *Times*. The Allies had just captured a pile of Nazi papers and among them was a list of Englishmen whom Hitler specifically wanted dead. Sagittarius, it was reported, was on the list.

At home, the Miller family liked to engage in argument for sport, always over literature, history, philosophy, and the like—in other words, always over subjects that had nothing to do with everyday life. Olga was the unchallenged champion. But not everything about Olga was fearsome. Her obituary appeared in the London *Times*, and I found the last few lines of it, dated February 11,

1987, on the web. In it she is described as "a strikingly handsome woman, elegant and charming, relaxed and well informed in conversation, hospitable at home, and always quickly aware of social injustice wherever she saw it."

As for Olga's religious views, my father doesn't remember any direct conversations with her on the subject. He recently described his parents as "uneasy unbelievers" but upon reflection thought that didn't really sound much like Olga. He was probably remembering Hugh's attitude more than Olga's, since Olga doesn't seem like someone who would have held any opinion halfway. Growing up, I remember getting a sense of Olga's attitude toward religion from my father; she was perhaps not as ardent an unbeliever as he and his brother Jon, but she was definitely an atheist nonetheless. So I've always pictured atheism coming down to me in a direct line from Johan Katzin, through Olga, and then through my father to me.

□   □   □

AN EMPTY HEAVEN

I don't recall any theological arguments within my family while I was growing up. We were all pretty much on the same page when it came to the nature of God and the question of God's existence. But we did all argue with my dad on the nature of *believers* in God. Dad was a physicist and never had any patience with people who held irrational beliefs, particularly when such people were discussed in the abstract—that is, when they weren't present. He was a bit more tolerant when they were personal friends and in the room with us. Then, if they were good people, he believed they were good people in spite of their irrational beliefs. My brother and sister and I—raised to argue for fun—felt this was too harsh. We believed that good, kind, and generous people could be believers, and they often explained their kindness in terms of their beliefs. The problem was that they didn't seem to understand that kindness can also be explained in other ways, if kindness really needs to be explained at all.

On my mother's side, my atheist roots do not run nearly as deep as on my father's side. Raised a Christian Scientist, a sect that prohibits the use of medicine, she never visited a doctor or took an aspirin before she left home for college. Abandoning her faith meant adopting a completely different image of the universe from what she'd been raised to believe. My mother is no coward (in spite of what she says). She breezed through ovarian cancer like it was just a bad cold. I remember the day she came home from her first chemo infusion. She lay on the couch in the living room with her family gathered round. The drugs caused sporadic aches and pains, which she told us she imagined as little battles taking place within her body; the drugs would find a bit of cancer floating around and attack. She recounted this to us almost gleefully. "Ooh! That was a good one." There wasn't a trace of self-pity or fear. During her illness, she oversaw construction of the house three states away that she and Dad would retire to, and she single-handedly packed up nearly thirty years of life from our large family house. Then, just months after her last infusion, with her hair only beginning to grow back in, she took a long trip to Europe, first to London to visit my dad's family and next to Lithuania for my wedding. And her chemo consisted of the same drugs that I got. The same drugs that reduced me to lying in bed watching *True Hollywood Stories* all day. When somebody reminds her now that she survived a very serious disease, she looks a bit surprised. "Oh. Well, I guess I did."

Though Mom's new world-view was vastly more realistic once she left the faith, and though it has kept her alive much longer than Christian Science would have, the change made her feel lost. She felt like she had no place in this rational new world. I believe the mathematician William Kingdon Clifford expressed how she felt when, speaking for new atheists everywhere, he said, "We have seen the spring sun shine out of an empty heaven, to light up a soulless earth; we have felt with utter loneliness that the Great Companion is dead." I remember her telling me, when I was no more than seven years old, that existentialism meant we got to choose the meaning of our lives ourselves instead of a God assigning some meaning for us. I distinctly recall latching on to the concept of *getting* to choose. How free it made me feel. But for her, having to choose a meaning for her life has been an unbearable burden. She said she would love to have some Divine Being relieve her of the task. Although outwardly Mom had been having the time of her life—studying at RADA in London, dancing in the chorus line at the old Copacabana, traveling Europe with the USO, and eventually landing a big part on the Great White Way—she has told me that inwardly she was in turmoil. It was Dad, a man who found joy in a godless universe, who came to her rescue.

□   □   □

WHAT I BELIEVE

WHEN YOU SAY that you're an atheist, you haven't said much that's specific about yourself. The word covers a wide range of different views of the world, from hard-hearted rationalism to wafty mysticism, but all it really says is that you don't believe in something you call God. I should take a moment here to specify the exact nature of my atheism—that is, exactly what I don't believe and what I do.

The word *God* means different things to different people (I capitalize the first letter because it's conventional). It's a word often defined in such a vague, all-inclusive way that it defies disbelief, as when God is defined as love, or as mystery, or energy, and so on. Obviously, none of these definitions define the God I don't believe in. Love and mystery and energy are clearly real things. Most people I've known who advocate such definitions I met in California, but outside of California people generally mean much more than this by the word *God*—and so do I. For God really to be God, it must not only have the power and pervasiveness implied by these Californian definitions, God must also have a mind. God must not be just some-

thing, but some*one*—God must be human
to relate to and talk to. God must think. G
God must listen. God must care.

This is the sort of God I cannot believe exists.

The universe is simply too capricious to be governed by
a God who cares, a God who sometimes creates visions of
spectacular beauty, of silken nebulae stretching across the
heavens, the silvery flash of fish just below the surface of
the water, a morning mist spilling into a country valley. If
all of life were like this, it would be very easy to believe in
a God who loves us. But the universe also creates moments
of unspeakable horror—I would make a list here but it's
not as much fun as listing the good stuff—and if all of life
were horrible, it would also be easy to believe in a hu-
man-like evil God who wants to do us harm. The universe,
however, visits these blessings and horrors upon us with
absolute randomness. Any attempt to make rhyme or reason out of them, any attempt to fit them into a model of
a caring, planning creature at all like us invites madness
and superstition.

The alternative is to ditch the idea of a caring, hu-
mane God altogether and become the kind of atheist that
I am. Though you might think of this as an act of disbelief,
I see it as an act of acceptance, an acceptance of the reality
of something that I suspect no religious person or mystic
is able to tolerate, something even more powerful than the
concepts of good and evil. Something that terrifies believers
more than Hell itself, terrifies them so much they can
scarcely contemplate it. Believers often tell me that I refuse

to accept the reality of God. It seems to me that the reality they refuse to accept is much more obvious and unarguable: the reality of the universe's complete and utter *indifference*.

Fundamentally, what I mean when I say I'm an atheist is that I recognize that the universe is absolutely inhuman and indifferent. Good and evil exist, but only within us. They are aspects of the human mind. The forces outside of us do what they do, governed only by the laws of physics and chance, unmoved by compassion or malice.

In other words: I believe shit just happens.

WHAT IS "I"?

BEFORE I CAN EVEN BEGIN to contemplate my death, I'm confronted by one of the most basic questions of all. When I die, what exactly will it be that is dying? What am "I"?

When I look inside myself, I seem to be a thing. I'm certain this is not an unusual perception. In fact, it's so common for us to think of ourselves as things that there's a common noun for these things: *souls*.

My soul feels like something that sits within my skull. It looks out at the world through my eyes, listens through my ears, speaks through my mouth, and animates my body. But at the same time, when I turn inward to examine it, I perceive it as something separate from these mechanical functions. I can easily imagine my soul being divorced from my body, floating around a room as part of an out-of-body experience, or going to another place after death. Indeed, such a separation is so easy to imagine that it strikes me as downright obvious. It's hard to imagine otherwise. Curiously, though, whenever I imagine such events, the mechanical functions of vision and hearing and so on manage to come along for the ride.

This obvious view of the soul as something separate from the body and the brain and the machinery of the senses is known in philosophy as *dualism*, and it's probably the first thing that springs to most people's minds. It leads quite naturally to the idea that when a body dies, the soul detaches itself and lives on somehow as a ghost or a spirit in the underworld, the afterlife, or in some sort of heaven.

So am "I"—that is to say, is my soul, the very essence of myself—a thing? An entity that might survive the death of my body?

Atheism per se doesn't necessitate an answer either way. There are many atheists who believe in some form of afterlife or reincarnation. This is not incompatible with believing that there is no God. It is, however, incompatible with the way that I think about the world and the way I decide what to believe in.

The point is, I don't find it necessary to believe something just because it seems obvious. Many things that are obvious are not true. It may seem obvious to me that my soul is a thing. But there is another possibility that would allow it to feel like a thing to me and yet be much simpler to reconcile with physical reality. What I believe is that my soul is inextricably linked to my brain. This possibility is known as *materialism*.

Many who dismiss the materialist view begin by misunderstanding it. To start with, they often preface it with a pejorative like "mere" or "simplistic." This is just an indication that the writer dislikes the basic tenets of science and is likely to prove gullible in assessing paranormal claims.

A more serious semantic problem is that people—even materialists—sometimes say that materialism means we actually have no souls. The implication is that our perceptions of our souls—things we see inside ourselves—are somehow hallucinations. This isn't what I mean at all. I believe that we do have souls. In fact, I don't believe the word *hallucination* even has any logical meaning when applied to such internal perceptions. As I understand it, hallucinations are caused by the misinterpretation of sensory input. But when I perceive aspects of my inner life, no sensory input is involved. So it is logically impossible to hallucinate your own soul.

What I'm saying is that my soul is completely real, but my first impressions of what it's made of and how it behaves may be wrong. To make an analogy: Outside my window as I'm writing, I can see several trees. They are unquestionably real trees. Yet I believe many of my impressions of them aren't strictly correct. When the air is still, they appear not to move, but I know they're still growing and moving at an imperceptible rate. They appear to be solid, but I know they are composed of the empty space between the atoms and molecules they're made of. Likewise, my soul, though real as a tree, need not be as solid as it appears to be.

Some define materialism as equating the soul with the brain. This is the wrong equation. A brain is a physical object that can be picked up and weighed. It can be put in a jar. As an object, it doesn't behave anything like a soul, and there really is no justification for equating the two.

The materialist version of the soul that I prefer sees the soul as the *activity* of a living brain. From this perspective, a soul is not an object, but an action, a sequence of decisions and behaviors, memories and expectations. It is not made of anything material in the sense that a tree is made of wood, and its physical form is no more mysterious than that of any other physical action, like a gust of wind. If you're standing on a beach, you can point at a wave and identify it as a wave. You can point to it a second later and identify it as the same wave. But it's not the same water. It is not the same object. Rather, it's the same sequence of cause and effect. Eventually, the wave runs its course and washes up on the shore. At that point it is over, leaving only echoes of itself etched into the sand.

About when I was born, my soul began. Since then, like a wave, I have splashed within my brain. I am not made of the same chemicals as I was at the time of my birth, but I am an unbroken sequence of cause and effect. The path of my soul is more prismatic than that of a wave, but it has the same kind of identity. And when it reaches its end, it shares the same kind of fate, leaving only echoes etched in the consequences of my deeds, and in the memories of those who knew me. To me, this picture is beautiful.

□   □   □

THE WONDERFUL BRAIN

ADMITTEDLY, THIS MATERIALIST VIEW of the soul is harder for some to swallow at first than the dualist view. Souls just don't look like this when we view them with the mind's eye. Many people have a particular problem conceiving of free will in the context of materialism, because if the decisions my brain makes are material consequences of the actions of brain cells, how am I a free agent? Am I not just a slave to those cells, particularly if their behavior is predictable? Personally, I see no problem with this. I say freedom is a perception, at the same level as the perception of the soul; it doesn't arise at the level of neurons. I see the freedom of my choices as being absolutely real, brain-cells and predictability be damned. Even if there were some very perceptive individual who could predict most of my choices before I make them, he might annoy me with his incessant "I knew you were gonna do that," but it wouldn't mean I wasn't making those choices freely. By the same token, if some future neuroscientist figures out how to predict my choices even more reliably, he might be even more annoying, but I'd still be just as free.

There is a strong reason for adopting the materialist view anyway. Centuries of brain research show that virtually every phenomenon that can be examined with the mind's eye can be modified by modifying the brain's function. Every memory can be knocked out by removing a part of the brain. Every cognitive skill can be impaired by damaging some area. Emotions and even personalities can be altered by altering chemical balances.

For most people the evidence that connects brain function to inner life comes mostly secondhand, from doctors and the web and perhaps books and TV. Beyond that, maybe it's also made up of some hazy memories of wild parties, confirming the influence of certain chemicals on mental states. So it was for me too, until the end of February 2009 when I had the opportunity to make a solid prediction in response to an emergency I experienced within my mind, and which was based on something I'd learned years ago in college.

Back in about 1985 at the University of Rochester, I learned about something called Wernicke's area in a neuroscience class. This is a region of the brain located just over the left ear, and in almost everyone it's responsible for many language skills. Damage to this area usually results in various kinds of language problems, one of which is an inability to find the words to express one's thoughts. In the beginning of 2009, I started whole-brain radiation therapy to deal with a multitude of tiny tumors that had metastasized to my brain. The radiation wasn't expected to cause any side effects, but nobody knew how it would react with Tarceva, the drug I was taking at the time. After consulting with several doctors, we decided I should stop taking Tarceva just before the radiation started. That turned out to be a mistake. After the first two doses of radiation, I ended up in the emergency room, unable to say anything more than yes and no. On the inside that day, I was thinking clearly; I just couldn't remember any words. The effect was the same as when you can't remember the name of the leading man in some movie. Everything was on the tip of my tongue, just out of reach. Luckily, restarting the drug, along with a couple of other standard tricks, got everything under control very quickly. I was able to speak again in days and was back at work in a couple of weeks. My brain function is completely back to normal now.

The punch line is that my doctor eventually showed me the brain scan that had been made on the day I was admitted to the hospital. Sure enough, as I had predicted, there was Wernicke's area getting mashed by a massive wad of brain swelling.

Well, the symptoms of the type of impairment that I suffered, Wernicke's aphasia, are easily observable from outside. They've been well known since long before I was in college, and many people suffer far worse cases than I did. But the point is that I experienced it *from the inside*, and when I expected to see something squashing Wernicke's area on the brain scan, it wasn't because of anything externally observable but because of an experience I was having within my mind. To me, this was a hard-and-fast confirmation of how closely linked my mental life is to the condition of my brain.

In the face of this kind of evidence, one at least has to concede that many mental phenomena—memories, language, cognitive skills, emotions, personalities, and then some—must be caused by activities of the brain, even though when observed from the inside that's not at all what these phenomena look like.

To be a dualist, then, you have to make a special exception for the soul. Dualists must view not only the body and the brain as separate from the soul, but the workings of the mind itself. The picture that arises is of the brain enacting virtually all mental activity while the soul sits off to the side operating the brain like a computer. But to the mind's eye—or my mind's eye, at least—a soul doesn't look qualitatively different from, say, memories and emotions, although those activities are clearly in the domain of the brain. What I mean is that none of them *looks* like the firing of neurons, even though I'm certain that memories and emotions are just that. It seems perverse to say that my perception of a soul is not the firing of neurons when everything else I see inside me is. So now it's the dualist picture that appears counterintuitive.

The only real reason I can think of for adopting a dualist view, at this point, is if you already believe in some of the paranormal phenomena it purports to explain, like ghosts and ESP and so on. But I don't trust the reports of such phenomena anywhere near the degree to which I trust the reports of how brain damage interacts with a person's inner life. When it comes to the extremely rare "unexplained" paranormal event, I'm prepared to dismiss it as an outlier or, more likely, something that was improperly investigated by overeager witnesses.

Actually, there is a second reason I can think of for being a dualist: Some people simply don't like materialism. Even if they don't already believe in dualism's paranormal implications, they just don't want their souls to be made of the same prosaic stuff as the vocabulary that's stored in Wernicke's area. They want their souls to be made of some sort of magical soul-stuff. On the face of it, a vain desire like this might seem a silly reason to adopt a belief about reality, but I'm convinced there's a deep conflict between believing what appears true and believing what appears comforting or magical. Let me just say that I actually like the picture of the soul painted by materialism. I think it *is* magical.

□   □   □

QUESTIONS FROM THE DEEP END

A M I DYING?
 No.

Of course, I will die someday. Probably much sooner than most people my age. But the way I see it, I am not presently dying.

From the moment I start reading a good book, I'm bound to finish it. But at what point do I begin finishing? When I'm on the last page? The last hundred pages? The last chapter? Past the halfway point? It's an arbitrary choice. By the same token, from the moment I was born, I've been bound to die. But at what point do I begin dying? It's just as arbitrary as deciding the point at which I begin finishing a book. Am I dying from the moment I was born, or am I living till the moment I die? Do I begin dying when a doctor hazards a guess that I've only a few months left to live? That's happened twice so far. The first time was more than two years ago.

It's important to note that doctors are often not very good at predicting how long people have to live. It's not a skill they want to develop. Not exactly a selling point. Nobody's going to recommend a doctor because she pegged

Aunt Millie's passing to within a week. Doctors would really rather concentrate on keeping people alive longer, whatever their life expectancy might be. And at the time of this writing (2009), life expectancy with serious cancer cases is extremely hard to predict because of the whole new range of targeted therapies that attack very specific details of cancer cells, which means they work in specific cases. It's hard to predict when they're going to work, but when they do, as in my—or more famously Patrick Swayze's—case, life expectancy soars way beyond the statistical median. The actor Patrick Swayze was diagnosed with stage IV pancreatic cancer in January 2008 and given just weeks to live. He had a dramatic response to an experimental targeted drug, was able to return to work for a year, and lived until the second half of September 2009.

So it's best not to decide that you're dying at the moment a doctor predicts you haven't got much longer to live. But even if the doctors are quite certain that a patient is near the end, because they've already given it their best shot and nothing is working, it's still not time for the patient to start dying. Randy Pausch, after being told, correctly, that he had less than a year to live, wrote in *The Last Lecture*, "I'm dying but I'm still having fun." He wasn't "dying" in the sense I mean it here. Throughout that book and the lecture itself, he was never "dying." He lived straight through to the end. And that's what I intend to do.

I've probably made this choice a few times during the course of my disease, always coming up with the same decision, but one time sticks out in my memory. It was early, before my first treatment began. I was taking a shower, and I started wondering whether I should just choose to die. After all, even though it hasn't been that long, my life has been quite an adventure. I've pursued at least the majority of my dreams, the remotely plausible ones anyway, and had some success at several of them. Struggling on for even a few more decades might not make such a huge difference. If it all ended in a matter of months instead, I thought, I could meet that end with few regrets.

Few regrets, that is, if I didn't have a wife and kids. They're the ones I want to hang around for. They're the ones I want to live for and keep seeing as much as I can. So that day in the shower, and each time I've thought about it since, I've chosen not to be dying.

However determined I am to go on living until the very moment of my death, that moment will inevitably come someday, and I can't help wondering what it will feel like. There are many different ways to lose one's life, and I strongly suspect they feel very different from one another. Having my organs gradually fail me over a course of hours would probably feel quite different from being suddenly eaten head-first by a giant crocodile.

□   □   □

NEAR-DEATH EXPERIENCES

One of the few luxuries of an incurable disease is that I can narrow down my thinking about this question quite a bit. I doubt I have to worry much about being eaten by a crocodile, or even falling off a building, or being hit by a car. I'm almost certain to go via organ failure, lying in a bed somewhere, over the course of hours or days. When wondering what it feels like to shut down through organ failure, there are accounts I can turn to that I believe are actually more than mere speculation, though I think most of them have been blown way out of proportion. These are particularly the accounts of people who have had near-death experiences.

Empirically, a true near-death experience goes like this:

1. A person suffers some sort of trauma, disease, or event that is normally fatal and falls unconscious. In most cases, this involves substantial organ failure, such as a heart attack.

2. The person enters a state that is, externally, indistinguishable from being dead. In my book (and this is my book), it shouldn't really count unless some medical professional verifies that the person's state really is indistinguishable from being dead; that is, a medical professional pronounces the person dead.

3. Then somehow the person returns to consciousness and often to full health.

4. The person reports memories of what happened during the near-death experience. For those of us who have not had them, these reported memories are all that we get to examine.

There's a pretty wide literature reporting such events, but many people don't believe they occur at all. In part, I think the problem has to do with what is claimed to be occurring. Many of those who write books and papers about near-death experiences do so as if the memories described by the patient are literally true. I am highly skeptical of this kind of interpretation. It is off-putting to people like me who like to exhaust simple explanations before jumping to wild conclusions.

However, some accounts have been related and studied by serious, skeptical scientists—Susan Blackmore and Karl Jansen, for example—who seek simple, neurological explanations of the reported memories. Their theories are still pretty rough, but I trust these researchers to get their basic facts straight, so I'm comfortable believing that the events they're studying actually occurred, as did similar events reported by others. I can believe there are people who have been pronounced "dead" by medical professionals, according to the standards of their day, who have recovered to essentially full health with collections of memories of what happened during their near-death adventure. I just don't believe their stories demonstrate any kind of duality between mind and body.

Another problem some have believing that near-death experiences actually occur is that most reports of them seem to be fairly recent, dating no further back than the 20th century. This raises the question of whether they're not some sort of recent invention of paranormal enthusiasts rather than something real that has always been happening to human beings. There are two answers to this. First, the 20th-century rise in reported near-death experiences could be a result of changes in medicine and medical reporting practices. Many near-death experiences result from CPR and related forms of resuscitation. These procedures have increased the number of people brought back from the brink of clinical death and thus increased the number of candidates for near-death experiences. Such forms of resuscitation only came into widespread use in the latter half of the 20th century, so a jump in reported near-death experiences around that time should be no surprise. Second, there actually have been reports of near-death experiences before the 20th century, though they are few and far between and mostly buried in literature. Much is made of Plato's "The Cave," which purports to describe, second-hand, a soldier's near-death experience that bears some resemblance to more modern accounts.

I'm also struck by how often the image of a tunnel appears as the connection between our earthly lives and the afterlife. Even the oldest written story known, *The Epic of Gilgamesh*, contains a description of a long, dark tunnel that Gilgamesh must travel through in his quest to visit his friend Enkidu in the underworld. It's conceivable that legends like this were inspired by reports of near-death experiences similar to those that are reported more frequently today.

A final point of contention with near-death experiences, and whether or not they really occur, is that there seems to be heated debate about whether or not the person is "really" dead or just, as Miracle Max would say in *The Princess Bride*, "mostly" dead. Some say that never coming back is a defining characteristic of death, so anyone who does come back after being declared dead must have been misdiagnosed. Others say that death is a physical state people can in fact return from, and this is precisely what's happening in near-death experiences. The distinction might be important for the purposes of those who want to impose certain mystical interpretations on near-death experiences, but it's not important for me. I'm just curious about what it will be like to die.

So, given the reports of these events that come from researchers who seem to be skeptical enough to be trusted; the simple explanations for why the reports increased in the 20th century; and the irrelevance of whether the patients are completely dead or just mostly dead, I'm pretty comfortable believing that there have been some genuine instances of near-death experiences, at least according to the purely external, empirical descriptions I gave at the beginning of this section. The real question is: What do the patients remember, and what do those memories mean for me? If the people who had near-death experiences went through almost the whole process, reached a point of being mostly dead, and came back, they still might have a great deal to tell me, even if they were never completely dead.

Most researchers and enthusiasts who have recorded near-death memories are struck early on by how consistent those memories are. There seems to be a fairly small list of experiences people have. Not everyone has all of them, and they don't always have them in the same order, but the list of possibilities is remarkably short.

I'll just briefly review one list based primarily on the work of Dr. Raymond Moody, one of the earliest modern authors to attempt a thorough survey:

1. A sense of being dead.
2. Peace and painlessness.
3. Out-of-body experience.
4. The tunnel.
5. The Light.
6. The Being of Light.
7. The life review.
8. Rising rapidly.
9. Decision about returning.

A question that naturally arises is whether the Light that many—if not most—people recall seeing is actually an aspect of external reality—that is, a passage to the next world, a glimpse of a Supreme Being, or a glimpse of the afterlife. I don't believe it is.

From what I've read, there seem to be several main arguments that mystics use to convince themselves of the external reality of the Light. The first is that, because the experience of the Light appears so consistently across so many cultures and times, it must represent something outside of human construction. But this conclusion doesn't necessarily follow.

When I was a kid, every television set in the world was made with a cathode-ray tube (there were no plasma or LCD displays). When any TV set was on and tuned to a TV station, it would display images transmitted by that station. When a TV set was switched from on to off—anywhere in the world, at any time—the image would disappear and be replaced with a bright dot in the middle of the screen. Eventually the dot would disappear, and the set would no longer have anything on its screen at all. It would be silly to conclude from this that there was some Supreme TV Station always transmitting a bright dot that those TV sets picked up and displayed whenever they were shutting down. In fact, the bright dot was an artifact of a universal technology, not evidence of some reality external to the TV sets.

By the same token, if brains all seem to create the same experiences as each other when they're shutting down, it doesn't follow that those experiences reflect some fundamental aspect of external reality. Of course a brain is not a TV, but it is a pretty universal technology. All brains in the world are made of neurons. Most human brains have the same basic structure. It is reasonable to think that, when various brains shut down—anywhere in the world, at any time—similar things might happen. Those things will be far more complicated than the simple dots on the screens of old TV sets and will likely form powerful experiences for the people inside them, but they will still be confined entirely to human brains. Thus the consistency of reports of the Light is perfectly consistent with my belief that love and memories and the experience of a soul and impressions of a Supreme Being are all phenomena confined within human skulls.

Now this isn't to say it's not possible that the consistency of these reports *does* reflect the external reality of the Light. I'm saying it provides no evidence one way or the other, and it's silly to claim that it does. As I've said, I'm more inclined to believe, on the basis of other evidence, that love and the soul and so forth are confined to our brains. All of these phenomena can be affected by manipulations of physical brains. So it's much easier for me to believe that they are all confined within brains and that the consistency of near-death experiences comes from the consistency of brains, rather than from the external reality of the Light.

If someone comes back from a near-death experience and reports some independently verifiable fact he or she could have learned only during the out-of-body experience or the encounter with the Light, then, unlike the consistency and apparent reality arguments, this would indeed constitute strong evidence that there was some kind of information input during the near-death experience. Unfortunately, I don't believe any such story has been reliably reported. I'm afraid that, not having made anything like an exhaustive review of the literature myself, I have to approach this issue in a somewhat ad hominem manner. I simply don't trust the writers who claim to have the evidence to support this argument. They don't strike me as the kind of people who will dot the i's and cross the t's to ensure that every alternative and more prosaic explanation of each event they report is unworkable. They seem to consider such work a chore imposed by outside "skeptics" who want to ruin their fun, rather than as part of the natural fun of real science.

There are at least three groups of people who have experienced negative near-death experiences. First, a group whose experience has been identified as a side effect of an old anesthetic once used to put women out during child-birth (this certainly isn't going to happen to me). Then there is the experience of the very rare, whacked-out, guilt-ridden believer in Hell (not likely to happen to me). And finally there's the experience of someone who fights to stay alive. In this case, the experience is similar to the pleasant experience of others but is interpreted negatively. It sometimes turns into a pleasant experience if the patient gives up and accepts his death before getting the "opportunity to turn back" (this could happen to me).

▢   ▢   ▢

AFTERLIFE?

The question that follows from all of this is What will it be like to be dead?

Remember what it was like for you at precisely 11:15 a.m., November 3, 1642? That's exactly how I believe it will be for me the moment after I die. And it will continue to be like that indefinitely. As far as I can recall, 11:15 a.m., November 3, 1642, wasn't a particularly problematic moment for me, so I'm not terribly worried about being dead, either. As Mark Twain said, "I was dead for billions of years before I was born and it never caused me the slightest inconvenience."

Of course, by definition, unlike a near-death experience, no one can come back from an actual, permanent death and tell me what it was like. Many people consider this an invitation to believe whatever they want. It is, after all, the Great Mystery—the Great Beyond—that we can never truly know anything about. But I disagree.

What Mark Twain believed, and what I believe, is a rational prediction, based on an extrapolation from real knowledge of how the brain behaves. We know that, in general, whenever a piece of the brain shuts down, a cognitive process shuts down with it, and the most sensible view of consciousness is that it's simply another cognitive process (even though the cognitive processes look like many different things when viewed from the inside). This means that by far the most likely result of shutting down the whole brain is that the whole of consciousness shuts down. The fact that no one can report the results of the full experiment doesn't change the overwhelming likelihood of that outcome. So I see no reason to believe in life after death aside from the desire to believe it for no reason. That desire, clearly, would come from an idea that some kind of afterlife is preferable to none at all.

Frankly, although I find it at first amusing to contemplate what some of the common afterlife fantasies might be like, none of them, ultimately, is satisfying to me. Let's consider some of them.

☐   ☐   ☐

GHOSTS

A great many people I've spoken to believe in ghosts. Perhaps the majority. Perhaps more people than believe in

God. But they do so to varying degrees. At one extreme, some believe just enough to feel uneasy in a dark room, or when a Ouija board appears to give a sensible answer to a question. (I confess I felt this unease when I was a kid.) Others believe enough to read and write huge books on the subject, build weird machines that detect "supernatural vibrations," and go on elaborate ghost-hunting expeditions in purportedly haunted places.

From an evolutionary standpoint, it's probably quite natural to believe that you're surrounded by sentient beings of some kind. The theory is well established and was termed the Hyperactive Agent Detection Device (HADD) by Justin Barrett. Consider a prehistoric man walking across the veldt. Some motion in the grass catches his attention from the corner of his eye. Two conclusions he can immediately jump to are that this motion means there's some kind of creature in the grass that could cause harm, or that this motion was caused by a gust of wind or something equally harmless.

If he jumps to the first conclusion, he's more likely to be wrong, but on the rare occasion that he's right, he's more likely to survive. If he jumps to the second conclusion, he's more likely to be right, but on the rare occasion that he's wrong, he's more likely to be eaten. If he's eaten, he's unlikely to reproduce, and any evolutionary benefits are put to rest. As Johnny Carson put it, "That's heredity for you. If your parents didn't have any kids, chances are you won't either." This scenario paints a picture of a hominid brain evolving over the millennia to become more and more cautious rather than more and more accurate. And this means that we end up hardwired to perceive sentient creatures—such as ghosts—with every creak of a floorboard or rustle of a window curtain or vibration of a Ouija pointer.

But here's what strikes me as strange: Though I've had many discussions with people who seriously believe in ghosts and who've tried to convince me to believe in them as well, none of these discussions ever involve the idea of *becoming* a ghost. In other words, most people I've discussed this with seem only concerned about other people's ghosts; they never seem to be concerned about being a ghost themselves. This phenomenon has been exploited in movies, like *The Sixth Sense* and *The Others*. We watch the entire films, identifying with Bruce Willis or Nicole Kidman, and it never occurs to us until the twist is revealed at the end that these characters, our on-screen alter egos, have been dead since the opening credits. I understand that certain Asian and African religions incorporate ideas of their own ghosts, but the Judeo-Christian believers I'm surrounded by simply never mention them. It makes me wonder if Asian and African audiences routinely figure out the ending of *The Sixth Sense*.

If ghosts are really supposed to be the shades of people who have died, then anyone who believes in them should necessarily believe they are a form of afterlife. And if I believe in ghosts, I would have to believe that there is at least some chance of my becoming one when I die. This is the most basic afterlife fantasy I can think of, so it's the first one I'll contemplate. What might it be like to become a ghost, and would believing that I might become one help me deal with the imminence of my death?

Since no believer-in-ghosts has ever tried to convince me that I might become a ghost, no one has ever personally told me what that might be like. Furthermore, I have little contact with any religion that takes the idea of becoming a ghost seriously, so my picture of what it might be like comes almost entirely from popular media: movies and literature.

Ghost stories divide pretty neatly into two groups. Most are horror stories, with ghosts of tormented souls who torture the protagonists in various ways, from simply scaring them to outright mutilation or killing. Clearly, unless you're a tormented soul yourself and have some people in mind you'd really like to torture, there's not much solace in becoming a ghost like that. It certainly doesn't seem like much fun to me, anyway.

In the other group of stories, the ghosts are sympathetic or even funny. The Harry Potter books and films like *The Ghost and Mrs. Muir*, *Beetlejuice*, and *Ghost Town* (in my opinion, one of the most underrated films of 2007) come to mind. In these stories the ghosts are much nicer, some of them even enjoying their afterlives. It can be fun to imagine myself becoming a ghost like that—floating through walls, horsing around with the living, playing little practical jokes.

But there's one problem that runs through each of these stories, and indeed runs through the pictures of the spirit-world that believers-in-ghosts have tried to sell me: Even the nicest ghosts have very limited contact with the living world. This is no surprise, since even the most ardent believers here in the living world have very limited contact with ghosts. At most, they may say they've seen a ghost once or twice, but usually they've just heard noises or "felt a presence." I've known none who had a long, clear conversation with a ghost, or played a game with a ghost, or even just spent an evening watching TV with a ghost. It's impossible, from this depiction, to construct a plausible fantasy of becoming a ghost that would seem any better than no afterlife at all. Everything I love is in the living world, and if this afterlife fantasy is going to grant me only tantalizing, intermittent contact with all that I love, I might as well not have the fantasy in the first place. To see Giedre struggle to raise two kids alone without any possibility of helping her, to see my daughters go through their teens without any possibility of guiding them, even just to see new board games come out without any possibility of playing them—what solace can I get from such dreams?

Sure, at least some fictional ghost stories allow their ghosts real contact with the living. In the Harry Potter books, for example, ghosts wander the halls of Hogwarts School of Wizardry and Witchcraft, interacting with the students almost as if they were alive. But stories like Harry Potter are not meant to be believable, and as ghost stories become more and more "realistic," they become less and less consoling.

As a dream of an afterlife, being a ghost can provide me solace only to the extent that it resembles remaining alive. In other words, it really just amounts to dreaming that I don't have to die in the first place.

□　□　□

REINCARNATION

Reincarnation posits the idea of an afterlife that actually allows me to dream of remaining alive or, rather, once again *being* alive. Whatever I imagine myself being reincarnated as—a higher- or lower-born human, a cow, or a dung beetle—I'm free to imagine I have full contact with the living world, contact I could never imagine having as a ghost.

Reincarnation is believed in by a great many people, even many atheists. I've known some folks who have come up with rather clever formulations of the idea. For example, a physics student I shared an office with early on at Bell Labs once told me he thought that over all the time remaining in the universe after his death, the particular atoms that make up his brain and body would someday reunite by chance, and he'd wake up as if nothing had happened. Others are hoping for a similar form of reincarnation when they have their bodies frozen in cryogenics labs for later resuscitation.

But for the majority of believers, reincarnation rests on its central role in the vast Hindu and Buddhist religions, where it is applied with a formal set of rules. Those who live their lives properly, in accordance with their karmas, will be reincarnated in forms preferable to what their forms had been in past lives; those who mess up and don't pay their karmic dues will be reincarnated in lesser forms.

This strict system of reincarnation might have a bit of a numbers problem when confronted with reality. The population of the Earth has been increasing for thousands of years, which means there would have to be some source of new, non-reincarnated souls in the system somewhere that I've never heard about. Well, the problem doesn't matter much to me. As far as I'm concerned, this is all just fantasy anyway. The numbers can be glossed over without affecting the fun.

And reincarnation dreams are definitely fun. In fact, of all the afterlife fantasies, reincarnation is the one I most enjoy dreaming about when I'm able to suspend disbelief. I can directly recycle every childhood daydream I ever had, and then some; I'm even free to dream dreams that would be impossible for me in my present life, like being the first black man to walk on the moon. (I'm a white man in this life.)

The real fun comes when I bend or entirely forget about all rules that might limit the selection of the next life. Why, for example, should my reincarnation come strictly after my death? Mightn't time be irrelevant to a soul between lives? This allows for truly wild fantasies, like coming back millions of years ago as a dinosaur. It also would allow for more poetic images, like the idea that there is only one soul in the universe, hopping back and forth in time after each death, weaving its way through time and space through every conscious being that has ever or will ever live. In this dream you and I would actually be the same person, divided only by the point at which we found ourselves on our soul's eternal journey through extratemporal reincarnation.

But as with ghost stories, there's something fundamentally unsatisfactory about any dream of reincarnation, a sort of mirror-image of becoming a ghost. If ghosts have too little contact with the living future world, reincarnated souls have too little contact with their past lives. I sure don't remember any past lives, extratemporal or otherwise. Of course, I might have one of those fresh, un-reincarnated souls that I suggested might be necessary to make the numbers work. But even people who claim to remember—and be affected by—their past lives generally claim memories that are so murky and vague I can't see the justification for any sense of continuous identity.

The point is, regardless of whether you take a dualist or a materialist view, a clear memory of who you were a moment ago is an integral part of your perception of your soul. As far as I'm concerned, if that memory becomes so unclear that I need, say, hypnosis to remember who I was before I was reborn, I might as well be living someone else's afterlife. A dream that I'm reincarnated after losing so much of myself is not really a dream of an afterlife at all. It's almost identical to the idea of my soul completely ending—which is what I really believe will happen anyway.

□   □   □

SEVENTY-TWO VIRGINS

Let's turn now to other classes of afterlife, those that take place somewhere far away from Earth. Probably the closest earthly place to the Muslim paradise for hetero-sexual males is the Playboy mansion. Like any heterosexual male, I'd enjoy spending a day or two there, if there were no strings attached. But what kind of asshole would aban-don his wife and kids to spend eternity there?

Several weeks ago, my daughter Fia and I went for a walk downtown. After visiting a bookstore, where she picked out two books I never would have dreamed of tackling at her age, we continued on to a music shop, a great place with bins of vinyl, used CDs, and shop assis-tants who really know music. As we searched for sheet music for her to play on guitar that would be interesting and also appeal to her friends, one of the staff engaged with us and ended up giving her a huge, two-volume book containing every song the Beatles ever played, because she can read music and he didn't know what else to do with it. I was filled with pride as we made our way home. How couldn't I be? My daughter, at ten years old, could do things I'd never been able to do my whole life. But it wasn't pride alone. I also felt a sort of security. This was a capable kid who could hold her head up straight and handle herself with a shop clerk. This was a kid I could trust to take care of herself, who'd be OK if I had to leave.

Then came the next day. For some time she'd been begging us to take her to a certain craft store farther than walking-distance from home, and so when we finally went, she knew exactly what she wanted and bought it with money she'd earned doing chores. It was a kind of kit, with a booklet and materials, for playing school with dolls.

It was all I could do not to break down then and there. All the security from the previous day vanished. How could I accept death while my older daughter still played with dolls?

So I ask again: What kind of asshole would abandon his wife and kids to spend eternity at the Playboy mansion?

□ □ □

A WORD ABOUT FOUL LANGUAGE

For the most part, I have tried not to be too crude in this book, but I've been talking about cancer here, and if you're not going to swear when talking about cancer, when are you going to swear? So on occasion when addressing this disease (or quoting Christopher Hitchens), I'll drop an F-bomb or some equivalent, and I can only hope it doesn't offend you. It's meant only to express the strength of my feelings.

I teach my kids to avoid swearing, because, as I tell them, they don't want to offend people when they don't mean to, and they want to preserve their power to offend people when they do mean to. Consider it: If you met the rapper Marshal Mathers and he greeted you with a stream of invectives, well, you might be ticked off or disappointed, but his use of foul words wouldn't add much to the experience, because that's just the way he talks all the time, right? But if you met, say, the squeaky-clean singer Julie

Andrews and she greeted you with a stream of invectives, you'd crawl into a corner and die. Julie Andrews is walking around with a lethal linguistic weapon, because she never swears in public.

Once I was at my doctor's office getting debriefed by one of his nurses, a fiery Brit named Jo. The phone rang and she received some bad news about another patient. She swore under her breath. I made her promise she'd swear like that if she ever got bad news about me. That was some months before I landed in the hospital with Wernicke's aphasia. I got some solace imagining her swearing when she got the news. I bet God wouldn't swear for me.

□ □ □

THE CHRISTIAN HEAVEN (AND HELL)

Unlike ghosts and reincarnation, there's no immediate plausibility issue with the Christian heaven, the one I have been most exposed to. As far as I understand it, no one is supposed to come back from the place for a visit, so there's no way to measure our dreams about it against any ghostly sightings. Perhaps an occasional angel might come to augur a miracle or two, but I'm pretty sure most souls aren't supposed to become angels, so that's not part of the dream. Once you go to Heaven, you stay there. Actually, I understand the story is more complicated than that. After Armageddon, God is supposed to create a new "perfect Earth," which will be in some way united with Heaven, and all Heaven's residents will move there. Whether God has any further remodeling plans beyond that point I don't know, but I'm sure the basic idea is to provide a sequence of Heavenly residences for those souls who make the cut. In any event, none of those souls are coming back to this Earth.

Before getting too deeply into a discussion of the Christian Heaven, I guess I should say a word or two about Hell. Hell is supposed to be an absolutely wretched place, and for centuries it's been imagined in great detail by artists, writers, and musicians as well as by theologians. And many people, I suppose, believe that I'm heading there myself.

But here's the nice thing about Hell, at least as portrayed by the most fire-breathing fundamentalists: the only sure-fire way to end up there is to disbelieve; for all other sins, true believers can always seek forgiveness and redemption. In some sects, all it takes is a well-timed ceremony and incantation. But if you disbelieve, as I do, then you're no more worried about going to Hell than you are about being magically transported into a Hieronymus Bosch painting, or reincarnated as an Untouchable in India, or being—I don't know—cursed to spend eternity running around in a Tom and Jerry cartoon, or any of the infinite variety of things you don't believe can happen. So for any given individual, either you disbelieve, and Hell is pure fiction, or you *do* believe, and you have a ready method for avoiding the place. Either way, Hell really poses no threat to anybody.

Actually, many kindly Christians believe that unbelievers can avoid Hell and get into Heaven simply by being good people. I even once saw a theologian on television try to needle Christopher Hitchens on the subject by claiming he—Hitchens—would make it into Heaven. Given that I myself generally try to be good, I take this view of more kindly Christians as an invitation to daydream about the place. Unfortunately, in comparison with the obsessive detail in which visions of Hell have been mapped out, Heaven doesn't seem to have received much attention. Those who write God-bashing books are particularly critical of this fact, saying that the serious attempts to describe Heaven have failed to come up with anything adequately appealing. They point to the most traditional, supported-by-learned-theologians image available and insist that it's pretty awful. This is the image of Heaven as a place of eternal praise, where the blessed have the great privilege of worshiping and praising the Holy Trinity, in person, over and over, for all eternity. Hitchens is scathing on the subject of the eternal-praise image of Heaven. He often likens it to North Korea, a place he has been to as a journalist, where there is similarly nothing for most people to do all day but praise their glorious leaders. After a heated tirade describing the terrible lives that North Koreans have to endure, he concluded the subject with the words "But at least in North Korea you can fucking die!"

In truth, the eternal-praise image of Heaven seems to require much more than a mere love of God and Jesus. I think you'd have to have the obsessive mentality of a stalker.

But I doubt the vast majority of Christians really look forward to the eternal-praise version of Heaven. I'm pretty sure I've never met one who did. Rather, most people simply regard Heaven as a place that's much, much, *much* better than here in a variety of ways. The streets are paved with gold. The walls are studded with diamonds. No one need ever worry about disease or poverty or loneliness or misery of any kind. It's easy to see the appeal of this kind of much-better-than-here Heaven, particularly if your day-to-day life is currently wearing you down. If you're sick with worry, the vision of a diamond-studded wall or two might seem a very nice dream. And I suspect it would be extremely appealing to those ancient desert dwellers who first dreamt of it and whose daily lives must have been extremely hard. To those ancients, in fact, the life of a middle-class family in a modern, wealthy nation would probably be a close approximation to Heaven. In Denmark, a country that consistently ranks among the best in surveys of happiness, people like to joke that theirs is the language that's spoken in Heaven. Perhaps ancient desert people would take that joke literally. Perhaps Denmark, rather than North Korea, should be taken as the closest place to Heaven on Earth.

But such simple dreams of Heaven strike me as short-sighted. Once you've gotten over the exhaustion of living an earthly life, how would you spend eternity? If I got to Heaven and all it had to offer were golden streets, diamond-studded walls, freedom from worry, and the Danish language, I can't help wondering how I'd avoid falling into eternal tedium. To make a dream of eternal life appealing, the image of Heaven would have to offer far more than diamond walls. I can't help thinking of Emily Dickinson's deeply despairing poem:

> I reason, Earth is short—
> And Anguish—absolute—
> And many hurt,
> But, what of that?
>
> I reason, we could die—
> The best Vitality
> Cannot excel Decay,
> But, what of that?
>
> I reason, that in Heaven—
> Somehow, it will be even—
> Some new Equation, given—
> But, what of that?

Some people expect that in Heaven there will be a complete revelation of everything—in fact, they may see this as Heaven's main attraction. They expect upon their arrival to finally have every mystery revealed; to finally learn in one blinding, ecstatic epiphany What It's All About—why we exist, the meaning of life, whether or not dogs go to Heaven—the answers to all the questions they have ever asked or never even thought to ask. This prospect fills them with joy, and I am sure they expect that the knowledge will in some magical way change how eternity feels, making it not just bearable but a delight. This vision of Heaven as revelation and epiphany is much richer than mere diamond-studded walls, and I can easily see how appealing it can be to people of a certain temperament. If you're the kind of person who is deeply disturbed by the unknown, who likes to flip to the last few pages of a mystery novel before reading the rest, you probably look at the prospect of having All Revealed as a great relief. Sometimes it appears to me that religious leaders and theologians assume all people feel this way, and they offer religion's promise to answer all life's questions after death as one of its main advantages.

But I have a different temperament. I am not disturbed by the unknown. In fact, mystery is one of the things I love most about being alive. Learning, figuring things out, inventing things—these are some of my greatest pleasures. But none of these pleasures would be possible if I already knew all the answers. To have All Revealed in a blinding epiphany would be a positively bad dream for someone like me. I can't imagine enjoying any form of existence, afterlife or otherwise, without anything to think about. For a dream of Heaven to have any appeal for me, I'd have to imagine there would still be mysteries in the place.

There's one more attribute of Heaven that I find the best of all the images I've heard about: Heaven is where you reunite with departed loved ones. In countless movies and works of fiction, this is portrayed as the only really important thing about the place, and I think they're right.

The tragedy of a death is that it breaks the bonds of love. To dream those bonds might be re-formed sometime in the future, someplace far away, is to dream that tragedy will be undone. Forget the presence of the Holy Trinity.

Forget knowing All There Is to Know. The nicest image of Heaven is a place sort of like Denmark, come to think of it, where you just get to hang out forever with the people you love. Even my need for mystery could be satisfied by this, because people are themselves mysteries. If Giedre were to join me in Heaven eventually, she'd certainly bring enough mystery with her to keep my mind occupied for eternity.

This version of Heaven is most appealing to someone who has lived a long or unlucky life and already lost some people most dear. The belief that death will bring reunion with those folks would certainly make it something to look forward to. My case, however, is different. My life has been short and (not counting the cancer) very lucky. Only two people I truly knew and loved have passed away—my mother's sister Colly, with whom I used to hang out when I lived in Hollywood, and my father's aunt Winnie, whom I often visited in Switzerland when I lived in Prague. My grandparents and a few other relatives have also gone, and I'd probably have loved them had I known them well, but I never really did. What's more, Colly and Winnie were both atheists, so it would be oddly disrespectful to dream that they're in Heaven. There is no one waiting for me there. All the people I love most are still alive, so death, for me, means not reunion but departure. My main concern is not those I meet up with; it's those I leave behind.

Particularly my children. It's a terrible thing to lose a parent during childhood, especially just before becoming a teenager. Giedre still carries the emotional scars of her mother's death when she was ten. How can I derive any solace from dreams of Heaven if they mean being dragged from my children here on Earth? What difference are Heaven and Hell to me if I know my own kids are suffering?

In *Little Book of Atheist Spirituality*, André Comte-Sponville suggests that in the initial stages of grief, believing in Heaven gives to those who lose loved ones a leg up over atheists. This may be true, but as Comte-Sponville points out, it is only temporary. And the cost is too high. Christianity bundles its afterlife fantasy with belief in an all-loving God, which invites my children to torture themselves with the question of why a God who loves them would rob them of their dad.

What matters most is not how I feel about my death, it's how my kids are going to feel. What matters is that the next day Fia can find me in her guitar and Ada can find me in her microscope.

□   □   □

MY LIFE SO FAR

THIS BOOK IS NOT an autobiography. Though I think I've led a pretty interesting life, I am not a celebrity and I haven't accomplished any famous feats. As far as anybody's concerned, I'm just a guy in my mid-forties who has cancer and doesn't look to religion for emotional support. A lot of my beliefs about reality come from my family background, but many of the details have been shaped by my own experiences over the course of my life.

Ever since I was very small, I wanted to be different from everyone around me. And I don't simply mean that I wanted to be a nonconformist. Nonconformists are all the same. I wanted to be completely and utterly unique. I wanted my clothes to be something totally at odds with fashion, conformist and non. I wanted to know things nobody knew, and to be ignorant of common knowledge. If you're at all familiar with American public schools, you know that my ambition made me a target for bullying. So during my earliest years of elementary school, while successfully pursuing my goal of being weird, I got beat up a few times and picked on constantly.

It didn't help that I took it upon myself to be a pint-size

missionary for atheism. Initially, through second grade, there were two vocal atheists in my class: me and my best friend, Greg (my best friend to this day). Then my family moved across town, and Greg and I ended up in separate schools. That made me the sole atheist in the room. But it didn't stop me from proselytizing like a madman. I remember one day after school, taking on half the third-grade class in a full-fledged version of what is called the Argument from Evil. The Argument from Evil goes something like this: God, by definition, is all-knowing, all-powerful, and completely good. But if God were all-knowing, he would know how to prevent cancer. If God were all-powerful, he would have the power to prevent cancer. If God were completely good, he would want to prevent cancer. Cancer exists; ergo, God does not exist. There are probably kids from that class whose moms still won't let them talk to me.

None of the isolation and teasing diminished my distaste for normality or made me change my behavior, but it certainly took a toll on my self-image. By the fifth grade I was a complete wreck, and during a conference one day my teacher turned to my mother and said, "One way or another, you've got to get him out of here." My folks responded by scraping together enough money to put me in private school, and I went to Gill St. Bernard's from sixth through ninth grades.

Gill wasn't the typical private school where students wear uniforms and compete for placement at Ivy League universities. Rather, I always thought of it as the school of misfit toys. This was the place for kids like me, who couldn't fit into other schools if our lives depended on it. Most of us were just weird. Some were truly nuts. A couple you could call bullies, but they didn't have the support of a crowd so were harmless. I even remember some friendly conversations with them. I also recall two truly legitimate athletes—guys who would have been top jocks at any other school. Now, jocks at public schools, even as early as fourth and fifth grade, had always been among my worst tormenters, but these two guys were genuinely nice to everyone. Man, that place felt like heaven. I didn't mind being comparatively normal or tolerating other people's beliefs there. I've looked Gill up online recently and should point out that it looks like it might be completely different today. Please don't judge the place by the description I give here.

Through all those years, before and during my time at Gill, my long-term dreams ran in the direction of film-making. At first I wanted to be a writer and director. But then I discovered the field of special effects, and soon I was reading everything I could about the likes of Willis O'Brien, Douglas Trumbull, John Dykstra, and Ray Harryhausen—special-effects experts for, respectively, *King Kong*, *2001: A Space Odyssey*, *Star Wars*, and countless B-movies. Trumbull particularly interested me because he went on to direct *Silent Running* and *Brainstorm*, movies I really liked. So that became my specific dream: to start out in special effects and parlay that into writing and directing films.

Then, during my final year at Gill, something happened that made my special-effects dream far more plausible but also opened up such unimaginable opportunities they would make special effects seem trivial by comparison. Somehow, Gill St. Bernard's acquired a Teletype terminal and an account on a computer at Rutgers University.

None of the teachers knew what to do with it, so one of them volunteered to lead a club. He picked out a textbook and put out a sign-up sheet for any students interested in trying their hands at computer programming. About ten of us showed up. The first few pages of the book had enough information for me to cobble together a little game where the computer would pick a number and the player would have to guess it. Didn't work the first time. Debugged it. Then it worked … and like a junkie, I was hooked. I stayed up all night reading the entire programming textbook cover to cover. The rest of the year I spent all my time writing reams of code that I'd type in after school along with a couple of other kids who'd had similar reactions to the machine. I checked all the computer texts out of the local library and read them too. That summer, the first home computers came out and I couldn't afford one, so every day I'd walk a mile to the closest store that sold them and write little demo programs. I was about thirteen years old, but this was clearly going to be my life.

□   □   □

BELL LABS

Though my dad worked at Bell Labs, it was one of the other kids in the club at Gill who learned of a group of high-school students who met at Bell's Murray Hill lab on Monday nights to mess around with the computers there. Each Monday the meeting would begin in a little room, where we'd hear various announcements and maybe a talk by a student about his or her project (yes, there were actually some girls in this group), after which we'd be escorted into offices where we got to play with the most advanced machines of the day. In this environment, I learned about stuff most of the world wouldn't hear about for decades—networking ... interactive text editors ... computer adventure games. I got my first e-mail address when the guys who started Twitter were still in preschool. One day, after I'd been attending these meetings for several months, the guy reading the announcements said with some embarrassment, "Um ... I'm, um ... I'm supposed to ask whether anybody wants to go on a camping trip next weekend." This was met with a combination of laughter and shocked snorts. Why on Earth would anyone suggest that geeks like us go on a camping trip? "Well, you do know," said our leader, "that we're a Boy Scout troop, don't you?"

Over time, kids in this group started getting hired as programmers by researchers at the lab, and when my turn came I got a job with a guy named Ken Knowlton, one of the early pioneers of computer graphics. Ken introduced me to Lillian Schwartz, one of the earliest computer artists. Lillian was best known for her work *Mona Leo*, which combined the Mona Lisa with Leonardo da Vinci's self-portrait. They matched up so effortlessly that she suggested maybe the Mona Lisa was a self-portrait. (Seems I've always been surrounded by heretics.) She hung around Bell as what they called a "resident visitor," and every now and then I'd code up some wild idea she had. Later, we were joined by one of my high-school friends, Wayne Loofburrough.

Around the time Wayne and I graduated from high school, Ken left Bell and the situation changed. As a resident visitor, Lillian had no budget to hire anybody, but she wanted us to stay on so hunted around for somebody else to foot the bill. The people she eventually found to do this—astronomers Arno Penzias and Bob Wilson, winners of the Nobel Prize in Physics in 1978 for having measured the background radiation from the Big Bang—were not looking primarily for graphics programmers, but they brought Wayne and me on to rewrite the software they'd used to analyze the data they collected from the sky, updating it to work with a new radio telescope that had just been built to replace the one used for their landmark experiment. The telescopes (both old and new) were not at Murray Hill but Crawford Hill Lab, a tiny place a good hour's drive south.

When the summer ended, Wayne left for college. I stayed. I had no intention of going to college. I figured there was no point; I was already reading every textbook I could get my hands on, I was already working with people most professors would kill to meet, and I was a snot-nosed teenager who was completely full of himself and knew everything. But this had been true for the last few years of high school, so my grades were, uh, mediocre at best.

I remember one day, I think it was after Wayne left, that the astronomers who worked with Bob scanned the sky with the new telescope in the frequency range of the background radiation. It was just a test, but they were re-conducting the original experiment. When we plotted the data using the new software, they pointed out the tell-tale spike that signified the flash from the Big Bang.

There I was, eighteen years old, looking at the echo of creation, using tools that I myself had taken part in making. Screw college. Screw Hollywood. Screw special effects. What more could I possibly need?

□   □   □

COLLEGE

What more could I possibly need? People my own age, that's what I could possibly need. That's what I'd left out of my calculations about not going to college. All the people I was working with most closely were in their late thirties at least. A few on the administrative staff were in their early thirties or late twenties, but people that age didn't seem to be in the range of a teenager. All my high-school friends had gone to distant colleges. By halfway through the year, I may have been intellectually stimulated, but I was also lonely. So I decided I had to go to college just to hang out with kids my age.

Of course, it wouldn't have made sense to major in computer science. That would have been a waste of time and money. Instead, I wanted to major in something I'd be unlikely to study on my own. A friend from high school had suggested I go to the University of Rochester and major in something called cognitive science. This was an experimental curriculum investigating different ways of studying thought: neuroscience, philosophy of mind, linguistics, logic, artificial intelligence, and a little philosophy of science to help us figure out how to tie it all together. This sounded perfect, and since Rochester was the only place with a serious program of this type, it was the only place I wanted to go.

It wasn't that easy getting in, given my high-school grades, but a little pigheadedness—I appealed the decision after being initially rejected—coupled with some letters of recommendation from Nobel laureates did the trick, and in the fall of 1982, I entered the freshman class of the University of Rochester. I did a lot better in college than I'd done in any earlier school, both academically and socially. I truly enjoyed my classes, which was reflected in my grades. I developed a tight clique of friends and even had a girlfriend for a short time. I made some money on the side as a teaching assistant for an introductory computer-science class and also by writing code to run a couple of psychology professors' experiments. And then, in the second half of my junior year, I experienced an important medical event that would serve as a precursor to events twenty years later.

Like any other college student, I spent my time burning the candle at both ends. Between studying and hanging out with my dorm-mates, I was usually lucky to get four hours of sleep a night. One evening I remember sauntering into the dorm lounge in the wee small hours. A *Love Boat* rerun was on the tube. Next thing I remember, I was being wheeled through the university hospital on a stretcher.

I'd had a seizure—grand mal, shaking on the floor, foaming at the mouth, the whole nine yards. For a short time I had to deal with the possibility that I had a brain tumor, but when the tests came back I was diagnosed as simply "seizure prone" (i.e. epileptic). Despite the seizure, I felt generally healthy enough to be flippant. When the neurologist said my EEG indicated that I probably had a lot of déja vu, I said, "Didn't you tell me that before?"

In fact, in my case the disorder turned out to be quite easy to control, just one pill per day. I had only one more mild seizure, a few weeks later, while we were working out the dosage. After that I went decades before my next seizure, and that one also occurred at a time of extreme sleep deprivation and stress.

When I graduated from college, I was ready to take work alongside people my own age. It wouldn't be at a place like Bell, though—the researchers there had PhDs and were thus still several years older than I was—but someplace developing software. Fortunately, Ken Knowlton had contacted me two summers before graduation and invited me to work with him at a start-up graphics company in Silicon Valley called Networked Picture Systems, or NPS.

□   □   □

CALIFORNIA

I arrived in Silicon Valley during a lull in its economy. The initial home-computer boom was winding down, with Microsoft/IBM having won the field and Apple coming in second. The internet boom was still more than a decade away. The first impression you get of the Valley, if you've never been there before, is that it's this vast wasteland of highways and fast cars and franchise restaurants. But that's just the surface. Underneath, it's actually the world's greatest incubator for high-tech companies.

Everybody was searching for the next "killer app"—the computer application that would transform the industry. After a couple of false starts, NPS placed its bet on desktop publishing. We were right about the application but wrong about the market. We thought we should be targeting professionals rather than home users, so we made a system that drove big expensive hardware like drum scanners and the laser plotters that make films for professional printing presses, rather than things like desktop scanners and printers. Boy, did Adobe clean our clocks.

I was lead programmer on a project to develop a page-layout system (something like the PageMaker program Adobe eventually came out with). I worked like mad on the thing, sometimes going as far as taking a computer home and writing code twenty-four hours a day in my underwear. As I recall, I was able to get an initial product out in a matter of months, but it still needed a lot of work.

After two years at NPS, I was dead tired. I'd also

saved up a good pile of money, because I earned what seemed to me a princely sum and I hardly spent a penny—I walked to work most of the time, shared a dirt-cheap apartment with a succession of friends from high school and college, and ate nothing but pizza. Before college I'd junked my dreams of making Hollywood movies, but I guess being so close to the place, and so far from AT&T's telescopes, reawakened them. Eventually I decided I should move to Hollywood and goof around pursuing my original dream. So I packed up with a couple friends and headed down to Tinseltown.

Those were good times. The three of us shared an apartment in the Beverly-Fairfax area, a part of L.A. so trendy they made a TV show about it. My roommate from high school, Phil, was an aeronautical engineer who would end up working on the space shuttle before I left. My roommate from college, Mike, was a grad student at UCLA studying human memory. And I just fooled around most of the time working as a grip on low-budget and student flicks, taking screenwriting lessons at the American Film Institute, and watching every movie that came out on the big screen. I'd go back up to Silicon Valley for three or four months each year to earn real money.

Then I wrote my first screenplay and showed it to a few people in the business. Though their criticism was constructive and they considered the thing salvageable, they made me realize that the story I'd written was just as dumb as the majority of stories to come out of La La Land. I mean, it included a reporter saying, "The people have a right to know!" for crying out loud. Meanwhile, it was the end of the '80s. Outside the U.S., Communism was crumbling. Western Europe was uniting. Everywhere, millions of people were taking to the streets and turning the world upside down. Everywhere, that is, but where I was. There they were on my television screen, and there I was on my couch. I decided to screw Hollywood. I figured it was better to live a good story and never write one than to write a good story and never live one.

□ □ □

EUROPE

My first stop was Denmark. This might not seem like the country of choice for a guy seeking adventure and fortune at the end of the 1980s, but I had my reasons. Admittedly, the main story line was the collapse of Communism farther east, but as a member of the European Union, Denmark would at least be part of the story of Europe in the 1990s. And I had ties there. My family had spent a year in that country in 1969 when my dad taught at Aarhus University while on sabbatical from Bell. So we had family friends in Denmark, and I knew it to be a safe place where almost everyone speaks English.

By a series of coincidences, I landed a job lecturing at Aarhus University. I wasn't remotely qualified, but my resumé arrived just as the graduate computer-science students were complaining that their curriculum was lacking in practical courses, and I fell right into the slot; there was clearly no way I could teach anything *other* than a practical course.

My time in Denmark was pleasant but uneventful. I learned the language—not that difficult if you drink enough beer—and my course was well received. But when summer came around I was ready to take some bigger chances. So I called up the Czechoslovakian embassy in Copenhagen (Czechoslovakia was still one country back then) and got the phone numbers for Charles University and Czech Technical University in Prague. The conversation I had with whichever of those universities I called first, as I recall it, went something like, "Hello, I'm an American computer programmer and I'd like to apply for a job lectur —"

"YES, WE'LL HIRE YOU!"

And I ended up teaching courses at both universities that fall.

When I moved to Prague, I learned I wasn't the only American cold-calling the Czechs to ask for work, and I wasn't the only one getting that kind of response. In fact, there were thousands of us, though I was only one of two who taught computer science; nearly all the rest were teaching English. My brother and sister, as well as my sister's then boyfriend, all followed me to Prague to teach English.

As great as my time in L.A. was, I have to say my time in Prague was better. I lived there from the fall of '90 until the spring of '92, just over two years in all, and used it as a base for traveling through the middle of Europe as I witnessed the final death throes of the European Communist system. Eventually I got low on funds and had to travel west to get a hard job for hard currency. I landed a position in Milan working on a specialized paint program for a silk-printing company. But I knew I wanted to go east. And I had an idea just which country I wanted to go to. And part of the reason for wanting to go to that particular country was a woman.

□   □   □

GIEDRE

It was on the last day of my first trip to Lithuania that I met her.

I made that trip while I was living in Prague, during some holiday or other. I'd visited Latvia, where I'd spent time hanging out with a beautiful blonde, and I'd traveled around Lithuania looking for my roots in Plungé and Palanga—adventures with another blonde on the train to Palanga—and now I was in Vilnius and had to figure out how I was going to get back to Prague in time for my next lecture. As all the planes were packed, I'd have to take a train through Ukraine to Prague the next evening. I was all adventured out and I was tired. This was my last full day. I resolved to find a café and just nurse a cup of coffee all day while preparing my lecture.

What ruined my plan was the old Eastern European custom of sharing tables with strangers. In that café all the tables were large, and I arrived in the middle of the morning when they were mostly empty. I sat by myself at a table for six or so, ordered a small coffee, and got out my notebook to begin working. Over time, the place began filling up, and eventually mine was the only table with a large number of empty seats. That's when four women came in—two blondes, a brunette, and a redhead. They sat down at my table and ignored me, as was the custom. Actually, I learned later that they weren't ignoring me. They saw my scruffy Eastern European clothes, cheap Eastern European haircut, and all-around slovenly appearance and concluded I must be Lithuanian. They were trying to give me progressively unsubtle hints that I should move. So their conversation, spoken in Lithuanian, which they assumed I should understand, went something like, "Don't you hate it when somebody orders one cup of coffee in a café and then sits there the whole day?" "Yeah. If he's not going to leave he should at least order another cup."

Meanwhile, the conversation in my head was going, *Dude! Dude! Check this out! They're all gorgeous! And they're sitting right here! Ya gotta do something! ... Oh, come on. They probably don't speak English. Lemme just get these lecture notes ready ... Don't be an asshole! You have all day on the train to work on the lecture. Look at the one sitting next to you, the one who's peering over your shoulder at your notes. She's got red hair. RED HAIR, DUDE! She looks like a sultry version of Molly Ringwald, except with green eyes! And she has a GAP BETWEEN HER TEETH!"*

I've always liked people with a gap between their front teeth. Greg has a gap between his teeth. The supermodel Lauren Hutton is famous for her gap-toothed smile. And my favorite athlete, Michael Strahan, has a gap between his teeth you could drive a truck through.

It was when one of the blondes looked across the table and said something directly to me that I finally spoke to them. I stammered, "Uh, do you speak English?"

"Yes," she replied brusquely and with perfect diction, "as a matter of fact, I do." At that point she still thought I was Lithuanian and was just using a few words of English to pretend I was a foreigner. This was a common way for Lithuanian guys to impress the ladies. She and her friends, however, were English students at Vilnius University, had studied English all their lives in a special prep school, and were well prepared to make such guys look like fools.

Of course I wasn't pretending, and once they realized I really was a foreigner they were more tolerant of me. When the time came for their next class, most of them took off, but the redhead and I ended up hanging out for the rest of the day. Her name, I learned, was Giedre Andrasiunaite. To anyone who doesn't speak Lithuanian, this is completely unpronounceable. The initial G is hard, as in "God." The following "ie" is pronounced "yeh" and has the accent. The final "e" is a sound I best approximate as simply "eh," but this isn't right and Giedre still holds it against me. In any case, all together I say her name g-YEH-dreh," which I think is about the closest approximation an adult American can make. Don't worry about pronouncing "Andrasiunaite"; it's not her name anymore, and it won't be appearing again in this book. She grew up in a big family: six kids by one pair of parents, and when her mother passed away from a brain tumor her father remarried, and his new wife brought a stepbrother into the home and later added one more half-brother. By various means, she'd managed to travel around Europe and the (still at that time) USSR. Giedre and everyone she knew, like virtually every Lithuanian in Vilnius, had participated in the demonstrations for independence just a few months before, and many had been in the crowds that were fired on by Soviet forces.

I went back to Vilnius a couple of months later, planning to investigate possibly starting a business there. This was how I hoped to participate in the end of Communism, by being a capitalist in a post-Communist land. I also hoped to look up that green-eyed redhead. This time I chased after her from day one. Her response to my pursuit was the most perplexing I'd ever encountered. Day after day, she never accepted, she never declined. I couldn't tell what was going on in her head. Of course, a guy never knows what's going on in a woman's head, but this was a whole new level of ignorance for me. For example, one evening while walking down a street I tried to hold her hand. I was used to a fairly clear response to this gesture; either the woman draws her hand away, or, much more rarely, she leaves her hand in mine. But Giedre responded by saying impassively, "You want?" I said, "Um . . . yes?" She said, "OK," and let me hold her hand. What on Earth did that mean?

Finally, after three or four days, and after I'd received endorsements from her best friend (who said I had nice eyes), her sister's newborn baby (who latched onto me at a party), and her brother's dog (who also latched onto me), Giedre suddenly kissed me.

For the next two years, while I worked in Milan and later back in New Jersey, earning the money I needed to start my business, we did what many say is impossible—carried on a long-distance romance. We wrote each other love letters. I visited her in Lithuania whenever I could. She managed to get Italian and U.S. visas so she could visit me in those countries. Long-distance romance is not impossible, but it is damned hard. We had many fights and missteps. Once, we got our signals so horribly crossed that we actually wound up traveling to the wrong countries, with Giedre going to the U.S. at the same time I went to Lithuania. (Boy, was Giedre pissed off when that happened!) Nevertheless, we were determined to keep things going, and we're both stubborn as hell, so keep things going we did.

In mid-1993 I felt I was ready to move to Lithuania. Giedre found an amazing little apartment in the middle of the old town, we moved in together, and I started my business.

□   □   □

COMING TO AMERICA

OK, here's the first thing I learned about business: You can't just "start a business." You have to have some solid idea of what this business is going to do. And it has to be a real idea in the sense that there has to be a market for what you want to sell. And you have to have some passion for doing it. And you have to be good at it. All this sounds rather obvious, and it is. So what does it mean that I'm relating it as something I learned *after* I started my business? It means I'm hopeless as a businessman, and my business was a catastrophe.

I won't go into details, but by the end of 1994 I couldn't continue without some source of cash. Luckily, at that time everything was still so much cheaper in Lithuania than in the States that I could go back to my old method of getting cash whenever I needed it by getting a consulting gig somewhere. For several months at a time, I'd go back to the place where I'd worked in New Jersey in 1993, a small research lab in Princeton that belongs to a large Japanese company. This meant that Giedre and I once again carried on an intermittent long-distance romance.

To make matters worse, Giedre had quit school and become an interpreter for U.S. military advisors, and that involved an increasing amount of travel. The U.S. had an office with maybe ten or so guys working to get the Lithuanians ready for NATO membership, and they employed a handful of interpreters. Giedre quickly proved to be the most popular. It wasn't because she was so pretty—all the interpreters were pretty—it was because her interpreting was qualitatively different from anyone else's. Where other interpreters would carefully ensure they translated everything with grammatical precision, Giedre would just barrel ahead showing no patience for grammatical niceties. Instead, she got the rhythm of the conversation right. She was the only one who could translate a joke and get the

laugh. As a result, she started getting all the choicest assign-
ments, which often meant flying to NATO conferences in
Germany or military bases in the U.S. with Lithuanian VIPs.

Though we were still determined to keep things going,
it began to get much harder. It wasn't clear just where this
thing was going. And my trips to work in the States
weren't the carefree jaunts of my days in Hollywood.
They were wrenching departures from the person I really
wanted to be with.

The lab I worked for in the States also began getting
exasperated. I was working on a contiguous project that
had to do with new DVD technology, and I was getting
more and more deeply involved in it. The lab's parent
company was sick of my regular disappearances into
Lithuania to lose all the money they'd just paid me. Finally,
on a day I was about to catch a flight back from the U.S.
to Vilnius, the head of the DVD project I was involved in
asked me point-blank how much it would take to buy me
out of my entanglements in Lithuania. I gave him a number
that for me was astronomical but for him was apparently
a pittance.

He just shrugged and said, "We'll give it to you."

"What?"

"If you move back to New Jersey and work for us
full-time, we'll give you the money you need as a signing
bonus."

I was floored. Suddenly I had three options: I could
decline and carry on the way things were, which would
certainly prove untenable in the long run. Or I could accept

and just leave Giedre. Or I could ask Giedre to marry me and take her with me to the States if she said yes.

By that point, I'd been with Giedre for six years. I'd never been with another woman for more than a few months. I was incapable of imagining the future without her. Clearly, option three was the only one conceivable.

She said yes.

Like everything in our relationship, our wedding was convoluted: first a ceremony in Lithuania—without benefit of legal papers because we hadn't managed to thread our way through the red tape in time—on an ancient temple mound, modeled after pagan rituals, with both sets of our parents present and followed by a huge party with our Lithuanian friends. Then a legal ceremony in Princeton, New Jersey, on the steps of a statue outside City Hall, attended just by my parents and a few friends from work. And finally another huge party in Manhattan, in which we re-enacted the wedding ceremony. As I recall, the whole project spanned about a month, and at the end of it we were well and truly married.

At first we lived in a small apartment in the center of Princeton. Then, in 1998, we learned our first daughter, Fia, was on the way, and bought a typical suburban house in the same town. It was big enough for the three of us and our second daughter, Ada, born in 2000. A couple of years after Ada was born, Giedre went back to school to pursue her life-long passion for interior design and graduated among the top of her class.

I've remained to this day with the same research lab

that paid me to come back to the States—they've been good to me over the years—and I've moved through several projects there. The DVD project eventually fell victim to politics, internal and external, and for a year or two I worked on automated face-recognition. From there I went on, ironically, to cancer research. Since about a year before I got the disease myself, I've been working with a team on the problem of getting machines to differentiate cancer cells from non-cancer cells in microscopic images of biopsies.

□   □   □

MACHISMO

'M DYING OF CANCER.

It's a surreal thought. Not easy to wrap the mind around. I was standing outside the doctor's office on the day I first heard the news, trying to get a signal on my cell phone so I could call my wife.

I said it out loud: "I'm dying of cancer." It still wasn't real. I wasn't in the hospital or anything. I was just standing on the sidewalk on a sunny day.

Then I thought, *Fuck that! I'm fighting cancer. I might win. I might lose. But until the last fucking breath—until after the last fucking breath—until the goddamned light goes out at the end of the goddamned tunnel, I'm fighting cancer!*

And then I blew a razzberry.

Of course, all of this was macho bullshit. I was still scared out of my skull, but I did feel better after that razzberry. I was ready to go psycho on the disease. When faced with an insane challenge, I favor adopting a certain level of insanity myself. Not so much that I can't do what I have to do, but enough that I can laugh maniacally while I'm doing it. So that's what this chapter is about; drawing strength from crazy macho bullshit. It was my first line of psychological defense.

Now, a word about the word *machismo*. It's a little ironic that machismo should turn out to be so important to me, a card-carrying nerd growing up in a liberal family where "macho" has always had decidedly negative connotations. From the kid who beat me up after school in fourth grade to George W. Bush strutting around an aircraft carrier in a flight suit, all the examples of machismo I've known have seemed moronic. To be macho meant doing stupid things just to prove you were a tough guy. What's more, machismo carries a certain cheesy connotation. More than "bravado" and way more than "bravery" and "courage," machismo connotes posturing. It's fake. It's TV wrestlers in stretchy pants.

The thing is, though I may naturally think of machismo and stupidity as allies, they are not inseparable. Sometimes it pays to be macho. I now frequently come face to face with clear examples of this. Dripping a poison derived from Amazonian tree bark into your veins for four hours, on the face of it, seems absurd. If this were proposed as a method of fraternity hazing, it would be outlawed immediately. But this is one of the things I have had to do to stay alive. Many people eschew chemotherapy in favor of "alternative" remedies that are not so harsh. But for all the fine words people use to explain how alternative remedies work, I put my faith not in words but in statistics. The fact is that chemo, statistically, works better. Besides, that Amazonian-tree-bark poison, Taxol, was itself once considered an alternative remedy. Now it's an alternative remedy that's been proven to work.

And in order to avoid dying, I need the same frame of mind that some bellowing lunkhead might need to avoid being thought a coward. So I've chosen the word deliberately. Machismo—in all its cheesy glory—is exactly what I need to get through the periods of the most intense fear, like those first moments outside the doctor's office.

In the original Spanish, "macho" literally means "manly." When my sister read an early draft of this section she opined that the word was too male-centric. Well, my response is that despite an occasional attempt to generalize, this is a book about my own experiences, and I am a man. So what I write is bound to be male-centric anyway—as well as nerd-centric and America-centric and several other centrics I'm probably not aware of.

Nevertheless, I'd argue that "macho" doesn't have to literally mean "manly" in English, any more than "sinister" has to mean "left-handed," as it did in the original Latin. If we choose, we can use "macho" for its chest-thumping, charging-into-the-line-of-fire meaning and apply it equally to men and women. I'd certainly call some female characters from history and fiction "macho": Boudica, Joan of Arc, Commander Ripley from the *Alien* movies. There are also flashes of machismo shown by women facing the same foe that I am. I wouldn't normally think of Fran Drescher (star of TV's *The Nanny*, who made a career off her annoying voice) as macho, but she titled her book about beating the disease *Cancer Schmancer*, which is just another way of blowing a razzberry. The cover of Marisa Acocella Marchetto's graphic novel, *Cancer Vixen*, shows a drawing of her staring down a female grim reaper and saying, "I'm gonna kick your ass!"

And finally, for sheer, blood-stirring bravado, few speeches can match the one made in 1851 at the Women's Convention in Akron, Ohio, by the former slave Sojourner Truth (as recalled by Matilda Joslyn Gage, who was present):

> *That man over there says that women need to be helped into carriages, and lifted over ditches, and to have the best place everywhere. Nobody ever helps me into carriages, or over mud-puddles, or gives me any best place!* And raising herself to her full height, and her voice to a pitch like rolling thunder, she asked, *And ain't I a woman? Look at me! Look at my arm!* And here she bared her right arm to the shoulder, showing her tremendous muscular power. *I have ploughed and planted, and gathered into barns, and no man could head me! And ain't I a woman? I could work as much and eat as much as a man—when I could get it—and bear the lash as well! And ain't I a woman?*

Sojourner Truth was definitely macho.

□   □   □

THE CHALLENGE

One of the foremost attractions of atheism is the self-reliance and courage it requires. As an atheist, I know I have to deal with my problems myself. There will be no magic help. Although it's not exactly a joyous feeling, I take a certain pleasure in this; a feeling that I'm a member of an elite group of people who have the guts to live without illusions. It's a sort of heroic fantasy, really. We atheists are the ones who don't start pleading for help from invisible friends the moment we find ourselves in foxholes. This is, in essence, machismo—a fantasy of being brave.

Many theists long for a Heavenly Father who will take care of them and let them be simple children again. Me? I hated being a kid. For me growing up was just a long, slow process of recovering from ignorance. I much prefer being an adult. I much prefer taking care of myself and corresponding with my parents as peers. My enjoyment of my "religious" atheist view is an extension of this; if there were a God, I'd rather earn His respect than beg for His mercy.

I know many atheists feel the same way I do, welcoming the challenge of taking care of themselves and living without illusions. But I also know that some atheists, like my mother, do not; for them, atheism is terrifying and dispiriting. It isn't that they're any less brave than I am. Rather, it's that they view atheism in a way that requires a great deal more courage than I think it requires.

The other day I took my kids to see the second of the recent Narnia movies, *Prince Caspian*. Near the end there is a brief moment I found quite compelling. The army of bad guys, a rumbling mass of beasts and armor, is charging to cross a river by way of a single bridge. As they thunder toward it, the youngest of the protagonists, a girl maybe eleven years old, walks quietly up to the other side with nothing but a tiny dagger. There she stands her ground, entirely alone. For a moment the world stands still; the armored mass frozen on one side of the river, held in check by the simple courage of a lone girl on the other side.

Of course Narnia is a Christian fantasy, so the little girl is not alone for long. Soon she is joined by the magic talking lion Aslan—the thinly disguised Jesus figure—who summons the full force of Hollywood's special-effects gods to smite the enemy with a huge watery monster sort of thing. To Christians, I guess, this is an affirmation of their faith. To me, it's just an affirmation of the wizardry of the digital-effects team at Rhythm & Hues (which I love but don't quite worship). The little girl's courage is reduced to a matter of knowing something the bad guys don't.

When we got home, I immediately sat my kids down in front of YouTube and looked up the video of the Tank Man of Tiananman Square.

It was 1989. Communist dictatorships had been collapsing all over Europe. The USSR itself was in its closing years. In the middle of May, tens of thousands of Chinese students and laborers began a series of demonstrations in Tiananman Square in the center of Beijing, calling for democratic reforms. The demonstrations went on for weeks. The Chinese government dithered and argued about how to respond. Finally, on June 3, they ordered in troops who had no ties to Beijing and brought the crisis to a bloody end.

In the aftermath of the attack, a news crew caught an extraordinary, now iconic image: As one column of tanks was leaving the square along a nearly deserted street, a solitary young man walked up and stood in front of the lead tank. The entire column came to a halt. For a moment the world stood still, the armored mass frozen in the road, held in check by the simple, solitary courage of a lone young man with two bags of groceries.

But this wasn't Narnia. This wasn't a Christian fantasy. This was the real world. And our guy didn't have a magic talking lion or special-effects water monster to help him out. He didn't even have a dagger. He delayed the tanks' advance for a couple minutes, stepping in front of them several times when they tried to drive around him, and even at one point climbing on top of the lead tank to talk to its crew. In the end, he was whisked away by some people who ran over to him from the side of the road.

It's hard to imagine the sheer bravery of his act. I've never faced a tank in anger myself, but my wife and many of my in-laws and friends have. They were in the crowd of protestors in Vilnius when Soviet troops opened fire. No news footage can show how terrifying it is. The sound, the smell, the mass, the sheer power manifested in those machines is not something you can see in the pictures. And the Tank Man wasn't facing just one of these things. In the famous AP photo of the event, you can see the guy holding back four tanks. But when you watch the video, you see that those tanks are just the vanguard. I count at least twelve, and it looks like there may be even more.

Few of us know anything about this guy or his fate. But I do know this: He was human, just like me. He was mortal, just like me. He cried when he was born, just like me. He bled when he was cut, just like me. He'd probably done some things he was proud of and some he preferred not to look back on, just like me. If all that is true, then maybe I can be courageous, just like him.

So the Christian fantasy is that they have a magic talking lion, and my atheist fantasy is that I am the Tank Man. With nothing but flesh and blood and a couple bags of groceries, he stood his ground before a column of tanks. If he could do that, I can stand my ground before lung cancer.

□   □   □

WHERE TO DRAW STRENGTH

The Tank Man probably subscribed to one religion or another. Most people do. As he stood before the tanks, he may have fancied that Jesus or Buddha was beside him, or that his ancestors had his back, or that some reward awaited him if the enemy struck him down. Similarly, Sojourner Truth was deeply religious. She's usually described as a preacher, and the rest of the speech that I selectively quoted from is full of Biblical references. Obviously Joan of Arc was a diehard theist. And many of my heroes—Teddy Roosevelt, Martin Luther King, Ernest Shackleton—were also religious. Does it really make sense for me to have atheist fantasies about being as brave as these people? Yes. The thing is, their religious beliefs are not what made these guys so brave. (Well, maybe in Joan of Arc's case it was—she heard voices, was probably schizophrenic, and literally did believe there was a talking lion, or some such, standing beside her.) But we have no reason to think the Tank Man wasn't sane, yet actions like his are far more rare than his probable religious beliefs. And at the convention where Sojourner Truth gave her "Ain't I a Woman?" speech, the men who were afraid to give women the vote—and the women who were afraid to confront them—were also religious. Their religion did not give them the courage or strength that Sojourner had. Sojourner and Tank Man and so many others like them must have had more than just religion.

When theists need strength, they draw on something they think is God. But if there is no God, then in fact what they're drawing on must be something within themselves. They're just not taking credit for it. They're attributing it to God instead. As an atheist, I believe there's something more to these people than they themselves believe. Whatever it was that made these folk such kick-ass people, it wasn't God, and it wasn't their religion. My fantasy—my atheist fantasy—is that just as I share mortality and blood and regret and clay feet with all my heroes, I also share those qualities that gave them their courage. Except, perhaps, for Joan of Arc's schizophrenia.

This atheist fantasy of being among the bravest that history has to offer is quite different from the theist fantasy of having a magic friend who'll make everything better. The theist fantasy, if it were true, would be very easy to draw strength from. If you know that the enemy troops are about to be wiped out by the talking lion's water-monster creature, it really doesn't take much strength of character to stand in front of them. The problem is that you have to really delude yourself to maintain the fantasy. You have to prop it up on a rickety scaffolding of faith and ancient rumors and tabloid miracles and special effects. And as soon as you witness one army crossing one bridge unmolested by any water-monster creature, the fantasy becomes pretty untenable.

To draw strength from the atheist fantasy, on the other hand, takes a lot more work. In fact, it's a fantasy of strength itself. But it's grounded in absolute reality. We can watch it on YouTube. It's a simple, undeniable fact that people can be fantastically brave. Real, mortal, flawed people, like me.

I guess this question is one of the things that separates theists from atheists. For an atheist like myself, the self-deception required to believe in the talking lion is just not an option. Even if I were able to doublethink my way into it, I'd forever be afraid of the crushing blow in store for me on the day that the frail scaffolding of faith came tumbling down. I just can't suspend disbelief past the point when the movie credits roll. On the other hand, I rather relish the challenge of measuring up to my heroes without the help of magic. It's not easy, but neither is doublethink, and I'd rather challenge myself to be strong than challenge myself to be weak.

□   □   □

MY TEMPLE

My best friend, Greg, once said to me, "The hospital is your temple." He has a point. Some people find hospitals dehumanizing, with the personnel constantly taking your blood or trundling you off to some huge white donut-shaped machine, but I don't. I think about the long hours those folks put in to earn their degrees. I think about where the machines come from—I know some of the humans who design and build them. And because I've worked on a diagnostic tool myself, I know that at least some of the humans who work on those machines think about the patients they'll be applied to and are pulling for them. *Humans* study medicine and figure out how to heal, and they build hospitals for the best of reasons. So I here submit my manifesto:

Why Doctors and Nurses Are Better than God

☐   **They answer when you call.** Imagine you're in a hotel room by yourself. You start to feel some pain in your chest and in your left arm. You know there is no question it's a heart attack. You manage to stagger over to the bedside where you find two things: a telephone and a Bible. Which do you pick up? I say you pick up the phone. The reason is we're all really atheists at heart.

☐   **They ask how you're doing.** Has God ever asked you how you're doing? It's a simple question, and in America it's the first question that anybody asks. And yet God never asks it. Neither do angels.

☐ **They speak in plain language.** If I need guidance and call a religious advisor, I'll probably get a cryptic answer. For guidance in plain language, I'll call the nurse.

☐ **They let you see them.** Imagine what it would be like if you were a true believer in Christ, and Christ showed up every day at your chemo sessions with no special prerequisites or conditions. He was just there every day, to hold your hand through the therapy. And when I say show up I mean show up in a concrete fashion: physically, actually there, not pretending to be there. Imagine how much easier it would be.

☐ **They don't work in mysterious ways.** Humans just get down to business. They don't screw around.

☐ **They'll always do everything they can to save you.** They'll fight to the end. God doesn't always do that.

☐ **They make you laugh.** The very first day I had a chemo session I was receiving two types of chemotherapy. I had to take them over a long period of time, injected very slowly to prevent allergic reactions. After the first couple of hours, I needed to use the bathroom. I asked one of the nurses, "How do I go to the bathroom when I'm all hooked up?" She looked up at me solemnly and said, "Here's what we do. You're sitting right across from the toilet. We open the door and you just pee from your chair."

☐ **They don't demand to be worshiped.** God says, "I am the Lord thy God. Worship no other Gods before me." Doctors do not say this. By and large.

☐ **They know what it means to be mortal.** God can't even share this basic aspect of human existence.

☐   ☐   ☐

WHAT MYSTICS MEAN

If you look at Sam Harris's website you'll find a lot of posts by fans of his work, but you'll also find some from those who are skeptical of his interest in meditation. Many people seem not to like the last couple chapters of his book, *The End of Faith*, in which he addresses the subject. At the 2007 Atheist Alliance Convention in Washington, D.C., Harris met a fair number of critical questions after giving his talk. Daniel Dennet got up and said, "They, the contemplatives, haven't produced anything useful." Harris's immediate response: "They might yet."

I think I have a basic idea of what's going on. It goes back to an experience I had in college when I spent a lot of time thinking about consciousness. Once, in the middle of the night as I was listening to Talking Heads, I heard a lyric that stopped me: David Byrne looks at his hand, opens and closes his fist, and says, "You may ask yourself, 'How do I work this?'" In those few words he expresses alienation from his own body, a sensation many of us have experienced.

Under normal circumstances we feel connected to our bodies and our possessions. But think about David Byrne's position. You can strip away your hand from your mind, and with a little more thought you can strip away your mind from your hand. You can strip away your possessions. You can strip away your sense of time. After a while you can get yourself into a state where all you are is the homunculus, the creature inside your brain that asks the question *What am I?*—perceiving itself but doing nothing else. I find the worst thing is being divorced from a sense of time. I got myself into this state of mind once, and it was a hell of a thing to get myself out. As I recall, it took several back-to-back *Love Boat* episodes before I could even begin to think minor thoughts again.

For several months I would slip into this state of consciousness accidentally, and it was not a fun thing. Eventually it occurred to me that I didn't have to go into this state accidentally, that I could go into it on purpose. The first time I did this was on a cross-country nonstop flight from San Francisco to Newark. I was staring at an exit sign and thinking about the shape of the letters used to produce the word *exit*. That got me thinking about how language developed and that for the most part languages are believed to have been developed first as creoles by children, and then as fully formed languages. This means that someone somewhere, sometime in history, for the very first time said the word *exit* in exactly the same way I say it now. So I have a connection with that person, just as I have a connection with the shape of the calligraphy on the exit sign, or the sound of the word, or the weaving of the fabric on my seat. Myself, the sign, the originator of the word *exit*, the fabric, the person who designed the fabric, and the machine that wove it are all one thing. In the same way that I can drop the distinction between myself and the sign, I can drop the distinction between myself and anything else, becoming one with everything else.

This, I believe, is what mystics mean when they say, "Become one with the universe."

□   □   □

INTERCESSORY PRAYER

How do atheists accept "I'll pray for you"?

Daniel Dennett had a very dangerous, nip-and-tuck, on-the-edge-of-existence emergency operation during which he underwent nine hours of surgery. When he was recovering, he wrote an essay called "Thank Goodness!" in which he makes clear that his "Thank Goodness!" is not a euphemism for "Thank God!" He was thanking the good in all the doctors, nurses, and technicians who rescued him and took care of him, and the thinkers who invented the machines and techniques that made his surgery possible, and the scientific institutions that fostered them. In the essay he ponders how to deal with people saying, "I'll pray for you," because for atheists that's a particular quandary. He stifles the urge to say, "Thanks, I appreciate that, but you didn't also sacrifice a goat, did you?" He writes: "But isn't this awfully harsh? Surely it does the world no harm if those who can honestly do so pray for me! No, I'm not at all sure of that. For one thing, if they *really* wanted to do something useful, they could devote their prayer time and energy to some pressing project that they *can* do something about." Well, look, you're in the deep end of the pool. You've got to decide whether you're going to sink or swim, and it's not easy. So Dennett's friends were offering emotional support in the form of prayers. What matters is the *emotional support* they're offering, not the intercessory prayers.

Here's a story from a believing friend of mine, Lori Madrid. She was suffering from throat cancer, and when she was first bolted to the radiation machine, she said that three Jesuses showed up, and she attributed this to the fact that so many of her friends were praying for her. But I don't think most grown-up believers view intercessory prayers as really having concrete effects, any more than Lori believed there were three extra people standing around during her radiation. More, prayer is an expression of heartfelt wishes from people who love you and can't be in the room holding your hand. Even for believers, then, Jesus is the messenger boy for these loving people; atheists receive the message directly.

So when someone says to me, "I'll pray for you," I say, "Thank you, that's kind. I don't really believe God has anything to do with it, but I appreciate the sentiment."

My parents regularly engage in intercessory drinking toasts on my behalf, raising a glass to my health each evening, in varying ratios of gin to tonic and vodka to vermouth. Now they even have their friends up on Cape

Cod drinking on my behalf. I don't really believe their toasts will save me, but it's fun to know they're trying.

□ □ □

MEANING VS. VALUE

My mother has told me that when, in her early twenties, she lost her faith in God, she was so depressed she could hardly cope. It wasn't the loss of a magical friend that scared her; it was the loss of divine meaning. This is the age-old problem of nihilism: the belief that if life has no *meaning*, it must therefore have no *value*. In the years after my mom's loss of faith she was drawn to the great 20th-century existentialist philosophers, guys like Nietzsche, Sartre, and Camus.

Now before I go any further throwing around names like Nietzsche and Sartre and words like *nihilism*, I must remind you that I'm not a professional philosopher, so I have no obligation to even pretend I understand any of this stuff. The truth is I haven't read very much of it in the original, and I can't claim I followed what I did read much better than I can follow the lyrics of an REM song. Most of my understanding of what these guys were about comes secondhand, from essays, written less eloquently but more clearly, that try to decipher these texts for laymen. It is a testament to the philosophers' opacity that those essays often contradict one another.

Here's what I'm pretty sure of: These guys, like my mom, were preoccupied with the connection between atheism and nihilism. Some, like Nietzsche and Sartre, believed the connection was inescapable, and according to certain interpretations of their work, they were deeply depressed by it. Others, like Camus, struggled mightily to escape from it and prove that life could have value even without God. The connection to nihilism also concerned philosophers like Kierkegaard, and he concluded that it meant that there *must* be some sort of divine meaning to life, a favorite argument of theologians. In an online interview, the theologian John Haught criticized the "new atheists"—Harris, Dawkins, etc., the guys I've been calling God bashers—for not worrying about the absence of a divine meaning of life, that they didn't feel the need to think out the implications of a complete absence of deity, that Nietzsche, as well as Sartre and Camus, explained clearly enough that the implications were nihilism. That's the basic gist of this stuff. I don't need to go into much more detail before I humbly submit to you that all this angst about nihilism is nonsense. There's no reason to worry about it.

My contention is that it requires a certain amount of courage to believe there's no Magical Being who'll help me through my problems, and I welcome the challenge of having that courage. But it does not take courage to think that life still has *value* even if there is no Magical Being who gives it *meaning*, no matter what philosophers and theologians might argue, assume, or fear. I like pizza. The sky is blue. Adam Sandler movies are funny. No philosophical argument, no matter how airtight the logic may seem, can convince me otherwise.

Life is valuable. It just is. I like being alive. Sometimes, when I get too deeply enmeshed in philosophical or religious discussions, there's a risk of forgetting this. Suppose somebody tries to convince me I don't really like pizza. It isn't the healthiest food in the world, after all. If there's no pizza nearby, if I'm only talking about pizza in theory and I'm not preoccupied with any actual pizza, my opponent might be able to make some headway. But if there's a warm, fresh slice in front of me, waiting to be tasted, wafting its scent into my nostrils ... well, the argument is over.

Likewise, somebody might try to convince me that because there is no divine meaning, life must have no value. If we're talking about life in the abstract, if I'm not preoccupied with the value of my own life—if, in other words, I'm still in the shallow end of the pool—I might begin to wonder. In the deep end of the pool, however, there's no question about the matter.

Before entering any discussion of the value of life (or the color of the sky), I must begin by keeping in mind that no matter how the discussion turns out, life will still be valuable (and the sky will still be blue). OK, keeping that in mind, then, I can think of three reasons that existentialist philosophy and theological arguments don't bother me at all.

1. Most of this stuff is poetry. Not real arguments. Even if there were an argument that could convince me to question facts like the taste of pizza, the color of the sky, or the value of life, it wouldn't look like the kind of arguments I've seen for nihilism.

In my line of work as a computer geek I often deal with

real, formal proofs. When these are published, the authors strive to be as clear as they can be. There may be debates about whether they used the right premises. There may be debates about whether their reasoning was sound. But if there are debates about what they *meant to say*, you know there's something fishy about the work. Yet discussions of existentialist "arguments" seem rife with disputes about what Nietzsche and Sartre and friends actually meant. This is not a property I associate with forceful reasoning.

I suspect this is often intentional. In *Breaking the Spell*, in a footnote, Daniel Dennett (who prefers writing clearly) recalls asking the French philosopher Michel Foucault why everything he wrote was so difficult to follow. Foucault answered that he wouldn't be taken seriously by his French peers otherwise. In a passage of *Thus Spoke Zarathustra*, Nietzsche has one of Zarathustra's disciples catch him in a self-contradiction. Zarathustra responds with a philosophical tirade on the importance of contradicting oneself.

Of course, much of what these guys wrote is thought provoking and evocative. Much of it is deeply moving. But being evocative and moving, as well as subject to varying interpretations, are characteristics of good poetry, not good logic. Good poetry is worth reading and thinking about. But unlike a solid logical argument, there is no need to accept the conclusion of a poem if it doesn't seem true.

2. *Logic itself is not infallible.* Even if someone constructed an argument for the connection between atheism and nihilism that was more logic than poetry, I would still look at it with suspicion, because logic itself is just a human

invention. A few of the rules of logic seem so blindingly obvious no sane person would object to them, but many have had to be carefully debated and fine-tuned over the centuries to yield conclusions that don't stray too far from reality. The ancient Greek thinker Xeno, for example, proved that it's logically impossible for the great hero Achilles to pass a tortoise in a race. Aristotle argued that women and men have different numbers of teeth. Fundamentally, logic is just a set of rules for deciding what statements should be concluded from what. Xeno's problem with Achilles and the tortoise had to do with conclusions drawn from statements involving infinity that weren't sorted out until the invention of calculus. Aristotle's problem with women's teeth is frankly a mystery to me.

One tip-off that someone's using iffy logical rules is when they begin to spout words like *inconceivable* and *unimaginable* as if they were synonyms for "impossible." This is a clue that they're not arguing the logical limits of reality, but rather the logical limits of their imaginations. This kind of problem shows up often in existentialist and theological arguments. They may not look like poetry; they may be completely clear and even boring, like real logic. But they're still just personal opinions (as is the bulk of this book), not statements of universal truths.

3. It takes a special kind of argument to claim that only divine meaning can give life value. I haven't seen even a poetic argument that a lack of divine meaning necessarily leads to a lack of value in life. Rather, that argument seems to be something people take for granted. They feel that if they can't think of any non-divine reason that life has value, then either it doesn't have value or there must be a divine meaning. Even the philosophers who believe God isn't necessary still believe it is vitally important to find some other explanation for the value of life. Camus, for example, starts out "The Myth of Sisyphus" with the following:

> There is but one truly serious philosophical problem, and that is suicide. Judging whether life is or is not worth living amounts to answering the fundamental question of philosophy.

Dude, OK, it's an interesting question, but there's no need to kill yourself if you can't find a good answer. More interesting is the part of his essay that comes right after that, where he discusses possible cases of *philosophical* suicide—that is, people convincing themselves to kill themselves through philosophical reasoning. All Sartre could find to support his thesis were works of legend and fiction. He wrote that he'd heard through rumor of one actual case of a crappy philosopher who committed suicide in order to draw attention to his book. It worked—people looked at the book. But they decided it was crap.

And even if you can't find a logical reason, it doesn't necessarily mean that life, in the end, has no value. Sartre never entertains the possibility of simply dropping the demand, saying that "meaning" is just a linguistic thing. Meaning is the relationship between a word and an object. *For life to have value it does not need to have meaning.*

Imagine living in a world where everyone believed

that leprechauns smoked pipes that emitted blue smoke, and this smoke, being supernatural, floated all the way to the heavens, giving the sky its color. This was the only explanation anyone had ever come up with for the color of the sky, and maybe it even made a certain amount of "logical" sense; at night the leprechauns stopped smoking and went to sleep, so the sky lost its color; on rainy days, the rain snuffed out the leprechauns' pipes and the steam filled the sky with clouds. You have a good look around one day, however, and declare that the idea of leprechauns is silly. "But you haven't thought out the implications of a complete absence of leprechauns!" a noted leprechaunogian might cry. "The implication is a colorless sky!" Well, of course the leprechaunogian is speaking nonsense, but you don't have to rush to come up with an alternative explanation for the color of the sky to say so. The sky is still blue. You might be alone in the world in thinking that you don't know why. But you'd also be alone in the world in being right about what you don't know. By the same token, most people believe our lives mean something to some deity or other, and that's why our lives have value. Frankly, I don't find this explanation of life's value even as workable as the leprechaun/pipe-smoke theory for the color of the sky. It then prompts such questions as What gives the god's life meaning? Does He worship himself? Not a very appealing quality, that.

Nevertheless, even if I grant that this is a workable explanation, and even if I cannot think of another one, nothing says this is the only possible explanation. Arguing that some story is a workable explanation of something is one thing. Arguing that it is the *only* explanation is a horse of a different color. As far as I can tell, the philosophers and theologians who worry about nihilism don't even seem to realize the difference. In computer science, it is common to formally prove that a given algorithm solves a given problem. It is far less common to prove that a given algorithm is the *only* way to solve a given problem. Such proofs can be constructed, but they have an entirely different form from just "Well, I can't think of any other way to do it, can you?"

So I'm perfectly happy saying life has no divine meaning, and life matters anyway, and I'm not completely sure why. Full stop.

Actually, I do have some vague ideas about why life matters. Pizza, the color of the sky, and Adam Sandler movies all have something to do with it. Not weighty stuff, but to me it's compelling. One of the problems I find with the writings of deep thinkers is they tend to dismiss the importance of trivia. James Watson, one of the guys who discovered the structure of DNA, put it nicely: "I don't think we're here for anything, we're just products of evolution. You can say 'Gee, your life must be pretty bleak if you don't think there's a purpose,' but I'm anticipating a good lunch."

□   □   □

SISYPHUS' JOY

At the end of "The Myth of Sisyphus," Camus comes up with an answer to his question about suicide, although it's not clear he was completely satisfied with it. I want to talk a little about that answer, at least as far as I understand it, because it'll get us out of all this depressing nihilism and back onto our real topic, which once again is machismo.

Camus starts out, as I say, by buying into the idea that life must have meaning to be valuable. He then goes on to define the "absurd man" as a man who demands that his life must have a rational meaning but who realizes that even if it does have a rational meaning, he'll never know what that meaning is. This is a depressing realization and puts one in an uncomfortable state of mind. The question that concerns Camus is how to go on from there. He discusses, and dismisses, a couple of philosophical ways to escape from the absurd state of mind, one of which is religion. He seems to think this demand for rationality is a fundamental aspect of human nature. I'm pretty sure it was a fundamental aspect of his nature, and probably the nature of the folks he hung out with, but it's certainly not part of mine.

Nevertheless, this absurd man that Camus is considering is a poor clod who's stuck with an irrational need for rationality along with a rational understanding that he'll never obtain it. This is a particularly bleak existence. The deck is stacked against him, and why would a sane person in that environment not commit suicide? Because I think nobody actually lives in that environment.

After describing various ways this person might live his life—as a hedonist, as an actor, etc.—Camus concludes by making an analogy with the mythical Greek character Sisyphus. For various crimes against the gods, Sisyphus was sentenced in the afterlife to an eternity of rolling a boulder up the side of a hill. Every time he got the boulder nearly to the top, he'd lose his grip, the boulder would roll back to the valley below, and he'd have to start all over again. This, thought Camus, was a fitting metaphor for the life of the absurd man.

Of course, real life is a good deal better than the punishment of Sisyphus. No matter what your life is like—and I mean you the reader here—I know for a fact that at the very least you have the opportunity to read something, even if it's only these words. And most of us have friends and reasons to laugh. Just this tiny list of comforts makes for an infinitely better experience than Sisyphus'.

Take football. Here is the real Sisyphus, and here he is happy. Consider the whole team is Sisyphus, because every season they have to roll the rock uphill. It's a titanic struggle. They start with a clean slate at the bottom, and as the season goes on they have to keep working at the stone, and at the end of the season, win or lose, having gone through that struggle, they have to pick up the ball and go through the whole thing all over again the next season. But if you look at their faces, they have these shit-eating grins on them. The players love it. This is truly Sisyphus happy.

But even in the extreme existence of Sisyphus, stripped to its most miserable essence, Camus ends up finding a reason to carry on. He focuses on the times that Sisyphus spent walking down the hill to start his meaningless task again, and what he sees in Sisyphus' heart is pure defiance. The ability to defy the gods, to stand up against all they can dish out and declare oneself strong, is valuable in and of itself. "There is no fate," he writes, "that cannot be surmounted by scorn." I think theologians aren't sold on this. In fact, Camus doesn't seem completely sold on it himself. He ends the essay with these famous lines: "The struggle itself toward the heights is enough to fill a man's heart. One must imagine Sisyphus happy."

This says what he means to say, but it sounds as though he himself has some difficulty imagining Sisyphus happy. I regard this conclusion as a bit of an exaggeration, but for me it is a *stirring* exaggeration. Scorn has definitely helped me surmount portions of my fate.

□ □ □

WALTER MITTY VS. RAMBO

I sometimes think of God as being Walter Mitty, sitting curled up in his Elysian bedroom, thinking about how strong and heroic he is, dreaming his dream of omniscience and invulnerability, dreaming that he's real when in fact he has no justification for believing he's any of these things, and I envision a realist Rambo silently patrolling the rest of the house and grounds with an AK-47 strapped onto his naked back.

Rambo is science. Like science, he's been on the battle-field. He's toughened up. When you send him into battle you can count on him, since he's been tested all to hell and back and has rarely failed. When Rambo/science returns from a new battle he may be wounded, or not even alive, because there's always some chance he'll fail (which sends believers into a frenzy of "I told you so"), but most likely he'll succeed because he's been tested so thoroughly.

Walter Mitty is a religious proposition. If he ever got into a real battle he'd be toast. And if he and Rambo ever met, I have no doubt that Rambo would beat the crap out of him.

I think both these views can be called fundamentalist in some respects. Religious believers will not go against their faith: Jesus loves them, and they're not going to question that, no matter what; they did not evolve at random, and they're not going to question that, no matter what. A scientist can take an adamant position on evolution, too, but it's not the same because he is going to question what he believes to be true, and if he finds evidence that it's wrong, he'll drop the belief. But the most likely outcome will be that, after questioning the truth of what he believes he knows, he'll find that what he believed was right, and he'll go right on believing it for rest of his life.

The problem you have when confronted with cancer is that you want to have *somebody* taking care of you, so you have to marry one of these guys, Rambo or Walter Mitty—science or God. Most people fall into a simple form of religious/scientific polygamy, where they have Rambo/science guard the house while they snuggle in bed with Walter Mitty/religion. With the assistance of doctors and nurses, as well as ministers, rabbis, and priests, they adopt complicated combinations of beliefs. In the doctor's office, they believe in evolution and the scientific understanding of cells and microbes, while in church they'll believe in creationism. When I see statistics that 60 percent of all Americans believe in creationism, I think those statisticians are playing fast and loose with the word *belief*. I think 60 percent simply believe they should answer "creationism" when they're asked that question. They must take care that Rambo and Walter Mitty never meet, for then the fundamentalist believer himself would have to beat up Rambo to protect his religion. In my own scenario, Rambo always wins, and therein lies a problem. What we want and what we need is solace, and Walter Mitty cannot provide solace if you let Rambo beat him up, so what to do? My answer: Rambo can provide solace too.

Scientists seek to understand the way that everything that appears magical is, in fact, mundane. This is "unweaving the rainbow." Whenever they have succeeded (and they almost always have), we the onlookers have a choice: We can see it as a flattening of the magical to the level of the mundane, or we can see it as an elevation of the mundane to the level of the magical. I choose the latter.

The great thing about elevating the mundane to the level of the magical is that it allows us to find magic in parts of the universe where we didn't realize it could be found: Newton's rainbow, the composition of the stars, the expansion of the universe, the Big Bang, the theory of evolution, DNA ... holy shit! There is more than enough

magic in one little molecule—acetylcholine is my favorite—to give you a sense of awe.

The mundane, by definition, is everywhere. When the
magical is *separated* from it, the universe can seem to be
composed of nothing but the boring, humdrum, everyday
things that are going on all over the place, punctuated
now and then by an infrequent miracle. When the magical
is *connected* to the mundane, what had been boring, humdrum, and everyday becomes a web of constant miracles.

Religious believers are in awe of some god or other. I
am in awe of the beauty and the magic of the universe. If
you ignore that beauty and magic, then you lose the solace.
But if you can hang on to it, it turns out that you don't
even need Walter Mitty.

There are many hard-and-fast scientific beliefs that
have centuries of evidence to back them up and that nevertheless remain amazing. The beauty of the *questions* and
the depth of the mysteries give you such a powerful picture
of the universe that you can't look at life without stretching
your sense of awe. Solace comes from that sense of awe.

□   □   □

MACHISMO IN PRACTICE

But enough of existential philosophers torturing
themselves in cafés in France. As a cancer patient, I have
real, physical problems to deal with. I've got frightening
news to hear and medical procedures to get through. Religious people can fumble with rosaries and recite prayers
to help them with this stuff. What can I do?

Part of what makes macho bullshit work is imagining myself as the hero of a drama. This means its application can be limited sometimes. It works best at extreme dramatic moments—moments that would be important scenes in the movie of my life. These are some of the hardest times to deal with in reality, but they're the easiest times to call up a pile of macho bull. On the other hand, there have been several moments that have been much less dramatic or dangerous, yet have truly worn me down.

Good candidates for applying machismo include stuff like spinal biopsies, brain radiation, chemotherapy, seizures—basically anything risky, painful, and above the waist. Of course these things can suck in real life, but they can be pretty glamorous in movies and TV shows. They make for good stories at cocktail parties, with awe-stricken guests turning pale and wondering how you ever got through it all (at least, that's what I like to imagine they wonder).

Then there are trials like, say, three straight days of anal leakage. Not many ways to spin that one and make it glamorous. You never see Hollywood heroes bravely soldiering through bouts of this shit on the silver screen, do you? And just try to impress the guests at a cocktail party with these stories. You might make them turn pale, but it won't be quite the effect you're after. It's way harder to get through this stuff on pure macho bluster alone.

I'm not saying it's impossible. This kind of below-the-waist, not-to-be-repeated-in-polite-company problem might not be the stuff of Hollywood and TV, but it is the stuff of many real heroic stories. War heroes, rescue workers, explorers, and all manner of people who have lived adventures I admire have had to deal with problems on this level. Hell, Lance Armstrong had to give a sperm sample less than a week after having testicular surgery. I doubt being religious would have helped much with that task. As long as a situation resembles any part of a story that I view as heroic, I might be able to summon macho B.S. to get through it, and I have occasionally sung Wagner at 3:00 a.m. on the john while … well, I'll spare you the details.

The times when machismo is impossible are the times that wouldn't be part of any story at all. The times when nothing specific is going wrong. There's no procedure to be done. No test result to await. No doctor's appointment around the corner. Just an empty room, a ticking clock, and remorseless uncertainty. The times that Anton Chekhov was talking about when he said, "Any idiot can rise to an occasion. It's day-to-day living that wears you out."

My nadir, up to the time I'm writing this, was not a moment of extreme danger, bad news, or even discomfort. It was just a moment one evening of extreme fatigue. It had been a year. I was beating the odds like mad, and I'd recently received good news from my latest round of scans; the disease was stable. The alarm from a previous scan appeared to be false. Life had been almost normal for several months. But I was having some minor digestive problems and my doctor suggested I should bring in a couple of stool samples. Collecting a stool sample isn't a big deal, but it's certainly not glamorous. At this particular moment, I was just about to collect the second one. I stood in the bathroom, holding the little plastic potty I was supposed to crap into, and I simply broke down. I'd been at this for a whole fucking year. All I could think was I don't want to play anymore. The theologians are right in thinking that Camus did not completely answer his question; it takes more than scorn to overcome this. But they're wrong in thinking that the only other alternative is a divine Friend who isn't there.

I didn't collect the sample that evening. I set the potty aside and did my business in the normal manner. Then I went out to the living room and found my wife.

My wife: my friend who is there.

□   □   □

MY 23RD PSALM

Curing one leper is a miracle; curing leprosy is medicine. I'm not impressed by miracles—miracles are one-offs. Believers can only hope for miracles because full eradication of a great evil, like smallpox or slavery or war or cancer, implies that the evil was unnecessary, which robs believers of their one sound defense against the Argument from Evil. This, if you think it through, means there is no God.

Atheists, however, have the freedom to truly hope. Humans, using their human brains, have made good progress. In medicine, many diseases that painfully killed people just a hundred years ago are now curable. We know how to clean up water and air, how to fly, how to talk to each other around the world, all by using our brains. We haven't done so well with war, but we keep trying.

So I propose an atheist version of the 23rd Psalm:

Yea, though I walk through the valley
of the shadow of death,
I fear no evil,
for I
have come here with an army of my kin
and I have Hope.

□   □   □

18966316R00080

Made in the USA
Middletown, DE
29 March 2015